"*Religions and Sports: The Basics* brings classic scholarship to bear on current cultural trends at the intersection of religion and sport in a digestible, yet thorough way. This text is a sorely needed primer on the burgeoning field of religion and sport—one that will help orient readers of all stripes to new techniques for understanding both religion and sport separately and in relationship."

Jeffrey Scholes, *Professor and Chair, Department of Philosophy, University of Colorado, Colorado Springs, USA.*

"As an introductory text for the study of relations between religions and sports, Shoemaker's work is student friendly in multiple ways: it features analyses of popular sports like pickleball and skateboarding; it examines religious orientations beyond those of monotheistic traditions; and it intersperses engaging research exercises throughout each chapter."

Joseph L. Price, *Professor Emeritus, Department of Religious Studies, Whittier College, USA.*

RELIGIONS AND SPORTS
THE BASICS

Religions and Sports: The Basics introduces the many connections and interactions between religions and sporting activities.

Readers will gain a foundational understanding of how to approach religions and sports analytically, theoretically, and methodologically. The book uses multiple relational frameworks to examine probing discussions around religious expressions in sports, the social connections of religions and sports, the mirroring of sport and religious devotion, and the discourse between religious ideas and leaders and professional athletes. Supplemented with numerous case studies and engaging exercises, it guides students through approaching research inquiries within the intersection of religion and sport for the first time.

With lively discussion on contemporary sports including skateboarding and pickleball, it is a must-read for all students of Religions and Sports and Religion and Popular Culture, in addition to sports fans more broadly.

Terry D. Shoemaker is Associate Teaching Professor in Religious Studies at Arizona State University in Tempe, Arizona, USA. His research focus is sport and religion in the United States, and he serves as the co-editor of the academic journal, *International Journal of Sport and Religion*.

The Basics Series

The Basics is a highly successful series of accessible guidebooks which provide an overview of the fundamental principles of a subject area in a jargon-free and undaunting format.

Intended for students approaching a subject for the first time, the books both introduce the essentials of a subject and provide an ideal springboard for further study. With over 50 titles spanning subjects from artificial intelligence (AI) to women's studies, *The Basics* are an ideal starting point for students seeking to understand a subject area.

Each text comes with recommendations for further study and gradually introduces the complexities and nuances within a subject.

EATING DISORDERS
ELIZABETH MCNAUGHT, JANET TREASURE, AND JESS GRIFFITHS

TRUTH
JC BEALL AND BEN MIDDLETON

PERCEPTION
BENCE NANAY

C.G.JUNG'S COLLECTED WORKS
ANN YEOMAN AND KEVIN LU

CORPORATE FINANCE
TERENCE C.M. TSE

FILM GENRE
BARRY KEITH GRANT

RELIGIONS AND SPORTS
TERRY D. SHOEMAKER

CRITICAL THEORY
MARTIN SHUSTER

Information Classification: General For a full list of titles in this series, please visit www.routledge.com/The-Basics/book-series/B

RELIGIONS AND SPORTS
THE BASICS

Terry D. Shoemaker

LONDON AND NEW YORK

Designed cover image: Getty – TuiPhotoengineer

First published 2024
by Routledge
4 Park Square, Milton Park, Abingdon, Oxon OX14 4RN

and by Routledge
605 Third Avenue, New York, NY 10158

Routledge is an imprint of the Taylor & Francis Group, an informa business

© 2024 Terry D. Shoemaker

The right of Terry D. Shoemaker to be identified as author of this work has been asserted in accordance with sections 77 and 78 of the Copyright, Designs and Patents Act 1988.

All rights reserved. No part of this book may be reprinted or reproduced or utilised in any form or by any electronic, mechanical, or other means, now known or hereafter invented, including photocopying and recording, or in any information storage or retrieval system, without permission in writing from the publishers.

Trademark notice: Product or corporate names may be trademarks or registered trademarks, and are used only for identification and explanation without intent to infringe.

British Library Cataloguing-in-Publication Data
A catalogue record for this book is available from the British Library

Library of Congress Cataloging-in-Publication Data
Names: Shoemaker, Terry D., 1976- author.
Title: Religions and sports : the basics / Terry D. Shoemaker.
Description: Abingdon, Oxon ; New York, NY : Routledge, 2024. | Includes bibliographical references and index.
Identifiers: LCCN 2023044679 | ISBN 9781032424019 (hardback) | ISBN 9781032424026 (paperback) | ISBN 9781003362630 (ebook)
Subjects: LCSH: Sports--Religious aspects.
Classification: LCC GV706.42 .S58 2024 | DDC 201/.6796--dc23/eng/20231019
LC record available at https://lccn.loc.gov/2023044679

ISBN: 978-1-032-42401-9 (hbk)
ISBN: 978-1-032-42402-6 (pbk)
ISBN: 978-1-003-36263-0 (ebk)

DOI: 10.4324/9781003362630

Typeset in Sabon
by Taylor & Francis Books

CONTENTS

	List of Boxes	viii
1	**Introduction: Why Study Religions and Sports?**	1
2	**Religions in Sports**	25
3	**Sports in Religions**	49
4	**Sports as Religions**	73
5	**Religions and Sports in Dialogue**	98
6	**Religions and Sports in Competition**	121
7	**Conclusion: Religions, Sports, and Disruptions**	145
	Bibliography	169
	Index	179

BOXES

1.1	Research Inquiry	8
1.2	Religion and Sport in the News	15
1.3	Insider/Outsider Dynamics	21
2.1	Professional Athlete's Religiosity	34
2.2	Religious Uniforms/Sports Uniforms	39
3.1	Scholarship Search	53
3.2	Converting Sports?	60
3.3	Geography, Sports, Religion	67
4.1	Initial Thoughts	76
4.2	*Homo Ludens*	84
4.3	Sacred Searches, Movies, and Disenchantment	90
5.1	Sports and Religious Conflicts	103
5.2	Social Media and Social Justice	117
6.1	The Spiritual Marketplace	126
6.2	Qualitative Interviewing Exercise	134
6.3	Quantitative Surveying Exercise	141
7.1	Framework Comparisons and Innovations	150
7.2	Calendars and Schedules	159
7.3	Pandemic Reflection	164

INTRODUCTION
WHY STUDY RELIGIONS AND SPORTS?

Why study religions and sports? How would anyone begin to analyze the relationships between religions and sports? What available tools and methods would ground a research project examining these two important cultural phenomena? As a sports fan, I knew of some religious athletes who made faith proclamations or simple religious gestures before, during, and after their games, but, in my mind, this was the extent of the relationship between religions and sports. I grappled with these questions during my graduate studies since one of my mentors focused his work on this topic. I was skeptical of the relationship since I maintained that most people operate in life categorizing some things as religious and, separately, other things as sports. For example, I do not know anyone who has ever driven past a Hindu temple and remarked, "what a glorious sporting arena." Why? Because most people simply know religion and sports when they see them. How could these two distinct cultural phenomena be confused? However, an unexpected experience provoked me to reconsider my position on this topic.

On a frigid morning in 2013, a colleague and I continued our tradition of completing a morning run while attending the annual American Academy of Religion conference. The American Academy of Religion is a large gathering of scholars who study religions, and the conference rotates its location in various cities across the United States. As the temperature was below freezing this particular morning, we decided not to run for time or distance but to find a quick point of interest. Our ultimate goal was to do a short run, see something interesting, and make

DOI: 10.4324/9781003362630-1

it back to the warmth of our hotel room. Since we were in Baltimore, Maryland, and staying in a hotel at the beautiful Inner Harbor, we found the Edgar Allen Poe gravesite a suitable place to visit quickly and return to the safe indoors. This would be a short one-mile run to the memorial and one mile back.

The Edgar Allen Poe memorial site rests in Westminster Hall along with several other historical grave markers, including American Revolutionary War generals. Westminster Hall is a formerly-operational Presbyterian church that is not open on Sundays for Christian services today but is available to be reserved for weddings and other special events. The historic church building was erected in 1852 on top of an existing cemetery. Although Poe's remains were originally buried in an unmarked grave in the rear of the church property, in 1875, through various funds, including a penny campaign from local school children, Poe was given a more prominent memorial located at the front of the church along with his wife and mother-in-law.

My running colleague and I made it to Westminster Hall that numbing morning and were pleasantly surprised at the historical value of the gravesites surrounding the church building. Hundreds of Revolutionary War and War of 1812 veterans rest within the grounds with historical markers providing some details of lives given for the development of a new country. We visited the Poe grave marker in the rear of the church building that indicates where Poe was originally buried, and then made our way to the front memorial. The chilly air forced us to move rapidly. As we inspected the memorial, I was impressed with the care and preservation of Poe for the city of Baltimore. The marble marker, standing almost seven feet tall, contains a relief of Poe's image and sits on a large foundation. As I stood at the memorial, contemplating the possibilities of frostbite and pneumonia, I observed something extraordinary or, at least, unusual to me. I noticed a vehicle pull up to the front of the church property; an individual man jumped out of the car, left the car running on the roadside, and quickly made his way to the Poe memorial. I noticed his attire was proper for the weather conditions: a thick coat and a large Baltimore Ravens jersey over the top of his coat. He stood in front of the memorial reverentially, paused, and then placed something small on the memorial. As far as I could hear, he said no words aloud. There was no making of religious signs like pointing to the heavens or making a sign of the cross like Catholics do. The gentleman then left as quickly as he had arrived. The entire event lasted no more than two minutes.

Piquing my curiosity, I visited where the Ravens fan had stood after his departure and noticed the coins he had placed on the memorial. At that moment, and I had not noticed this beforehand, I saw several coins littering the ground, having fallen off of the Poe memorial. While inspecting the site anew, a second car pulled up to the front of the church property. Two Ravens fans performed something similar to the first fan at the Poe memorial. Also wearing Ravens jerseys and depositing a few coins at the memorial after a brief moment of reverence, these fans simply left the premises after completing their…what? Ritual? Although I truly wanted to stay at the site to see if more Ravens fans showed up, the frigid conditions compelled my colleague and I to vacate the premises and run back to our hotel room.

Later that day, I spent time conducting Internet searches about the Poe memorial and Westminster Hall, its relation to the Baltimore Ravens, and this unusual practice. I discovered that, in 1996, the Baltimore football organization adopted Ravens as their team's name after Poe's famous poem "The Raven." The fans' practice at the memorial site earlier that morning echoed the early pennies for Poe campaign by the school children in order to pay respect to Poe and potentially receive some good luck for their football team. This activity may have worked since later that Sunday afternoon the Ravens defeated the New York Jets in the cold conditions with a final score of 19-3.

What struck me most during that experience was the context: sports fans paid ritualized respect to their team on a Sunday morning at a church property no longer operational for religious services. Had I observed a religious ritual that morning consisting of a poet's memorial and football fans performing a superstitious act to propel their team to victory? Or was this simply a practice by some eccentric Ravens fans having little to do with religious expression? What about me, as the observer, in that moment – what was I to make of this as a scholar of religion? These observations significantly blurred the lines in my thinking about the categories of religions and sports.

RELIGIOUS STUDIES AND SPORTS

The questions raised in the Ravens memorializing Edgar Allen Poe case study are complicated, to say the least. Fortunately, religious studies offers ways to approach these questions, provide a rich analysis, and then construct theories about various phenomena in our world. For those unfamiliar, religious studies is an academic discipline like sociology or economics. Scholars of religious studies examine, analyze, and debate issues regarding human activities focusing on religious rituals, behaviors, beliefs, practices, and institutions. I received my training in the field of religious studies, and it is worthwhile to think about how religious studies can aid in understanding sporting phenomena in the world and to respond to lingering questions such as the Ravens fans and Poe example.

Religious studies is an academic field of researchers devoted to understanding and explaining religious phenomena throughout history and the contemporary world. This means that in our venture to understand religion better, religious studies provides us with a rich body of knowledge with which we can engage. This field of research supplies various types of data, case studies, and debates. For instance, if you want to know more about the ancient Arabian religious tradition of Zoroastrianism and the number of affiliates of Zoroastrianism today, then scholarship within religious studies is a great resource. Or suppose your interests were very specific, like you wanted to know about the lives of boy monks within Buddhist monasteries in Sri Lanka. In that case, you might check out religious studies scholar, Jeffrey Samuels' (2010) *Attracting the Heart*. The field is vast, with scholars across the globe studying, analyzing, and theorizing about religion in the past, today, and in the future.

One of the key aspects of religious studies is the field's multidisciplinary nature. This means that religious studies is composed of various methodological approaches used to answer questions regarding religion. These methodologies include sociological, anthropological, historical, textual, philosophical, and gender studies approaches, along with a host of others, which are used to analyze case studies and theorize religion. As religion is a human activity, one single methodological approach typically provides only a partial response to research questions. Within religious studies, then, there are both quantitative and qualitative approaches to engaging case studies of religions. Quantitative studies are those numerically-based studies, often measuring larger data sets. For instance, Pew Research Foundation and PRRI (Public Religion Research Institute) provide a wide variety of quantitative survey data conducted in order to get a broad view of religious affiliations, perspectives, and changes. Those employing quantitative approaches often construct surveys to gain a broad understanding of perspectives, attitudes, and positions. Once surveying meets the target number of responses, quantitative scholars analyze the data with in-depth statistical processes. These sources are ideal for getting a better grasp on how many Germans identify as Muslim and how this changed over the years, for example. Quantitatively, religion can be counted and measured to account for affiliations, number of adherents, increases and decreases in participation, or public opinions on specific topics designated as religious. These studies contribute significantly to a broad understanding of religion across countries and continents.

Qualitative research, another key aspect of religious studies, typically offers a finer, on-the-ground perspective of religion and how religion operates in the world. Whereas a quantitative survey might indicate an increase in religious disaffiliation, a qualitative study could supply a thick description of what it looks like to live as a person leaving religious commitment behind. For example, Christel Manning's (2015) *Losing Our Religion: How Unaffiliated Parents are Raising Their Children* provides accounts of individuals who decided to leave their original religious affiliation and what life looks like for these people today, specifically with regard to child rearing. Qualitative studies often rely on participant observations and interviews with individuals and/or focus groups to offer different angles into case studies. Interviewing techniques vary but provide on-the-ground perspectives, individual histories, and capture the lived experiences of individuals within communities. Combined, the qualitative and quantitative research in religious studies paints a fuller picture, though not a complete picture, of religions and lived religion. These research projects also build upon the archaeological and historical archiving conducted by other religious studies scholars.

The discourse within religious studies – those debates and discussions about theories, data, and case studies – also propels the field of research further. This is the purpose of the empirical method. As more knowledge is generated, it creates the need for further research projects, which, in turn, forces a reconsideration and honing of theoretical frameworks. Over the last decades, the field of religious studies continues to grapple with its colonial roots and whether "religion" as a term and category can be universally applied across the globe. This focus forced religious studies scholars to reconsider definitional approaches – those studies seeking to define, once and for all, what religion actually is – to the study of religion. Also in question were the earliest, Western approaches working from an assumption that Christianity was the flagship religion from which to construct a definition and then deploy that definition to other cultural practices that may or may not look like Christian practices. This tremendous inward critique pushes those within religious studies to be more careful regarding what is considered religion. In some instances, the definitions of religion were simply too broad to be useful. In other instances, the definitions of religion were too narrow and excluded some cultural practices mirroring religiosity.

Within the field of religious studies, certain works catapult the field into new directions. Thomas Luckman's *The Invisible Religion*, published in the 1960s, propelled religious studies scholars to move beyond institutional religion. In his work, Luckman argued that simply analyzing religious practices found within institutions significantly restricted the scope of several projects and theories. Instead, Luckman recognized a turn to individuality within Western societies forming a private sphere of meaning making. These more privatized forms of religiosities find affirmation with family systems and other types of social networks, again, beyond religious institutions. Luckman's overall argument concedes a gap in the field of religion data. This move to think beyond institutionalized and organized religion advanced the disciplinary field of religious studies. Responding to Luckman, many scholars focus their interests on individual religious and/or spiritual rituals, new religious movements outside of traditionally recognized religious institutions, and they are more attentive to the role of power dynamics within religion.

Taking Luckman's critique and the variety of methodologies of religious studies, it is a simple move to begin questioning what should be considered religious phenomena. If a parent does not attend or affiliate with a religious organization but finds deep meaning in the birth of a child and performs a dedication, does that count as a religious practice? Does religion influence other aspects of individual life like economic decisions or travel planning? Can we describe an individual's commitment to a film series or fandom (think *Harry Potter* or *Star Wars*) as religious devotion? Must what qualifies as religion include a deity or is this a Western definition (undergirded with Christian ideas) impeding scholarship? These are a small sampling of the kinds of deep questions circulating in scholarly discussions.

This quick review of how religious studies approaches research inquiries shows how religious studies could help direct our questions regarding the Ravens fans' actions mentioned at the beginning of this chapter. Variously trained religious studies scholars would undoubtedly approach this question differently. A psychologist of religion might be interested in the subjective wellbeing of Ravens fans. This psychologist might construct a study to examine the question of life satisfaction for Ravens fans who participate in the Poe ritual. Are Ravens fans happier before, during, and after the game if they visit the Poe memorial? A sociologist of religion might want to quantify the research. How many Ravens fans stop on an average game day? How does this compare to other American football team fans or other sports? An anthropologist of religion might want to observe these activities in much more detail and ask these Ravens fans in-depth questions about their practices like: How long have they been participating in this act? What are the important aspects of the practice? Does this practice help the Ravens win? Does it give the fan a way to feel like they are contributing to their team's success? Of course, a historian of religion would dive into the history of the church building and usage, the transferring of Poe's body to the current location, and the naming of the Ravens after Poe's famous poem. Does this history generate the current practices of memorializing Poe? If so, how? Have the practices changed over time? If so, how and why? As can be seen, religious studies, as an academic discipline, is equipped to analyze several angles of the

Ravens/Poe phenomenon. Collectively, these studies could provide substantive theories and understandings of this ritual.

Over the last decades, numerous religious studies scholars, including many of my colleagues, have approached the topics of religions and sports employing various methods and approaches of religious studies. Their work lays a strong foundation for understanding the relationship between religions and sports historically and in contemporary society. This includes numerous case studies, theories, and methodological approaches aiding in a broad examination of religions and sports across the globe. Throughout this book, I'll draw upon work conducted primarily in the subfield of religion and sport while also depending on some work outside of religious studies.

> **BOX 1.1 RESEARCH INQUIRY**
>
> Now that the reader has a better grasp of religious studies, some of its methodologies, and some of the various questions religious studies scholars might ask, let's take a stab at creating a hypothetical research question and approach.
>
> Often a research question is called a research problem or inquiry. A research problem or inquiry is a specific issue that a research project is trying to resolve or explore. The primary research question guides the research project, narrows down the scope of the project, and helps the researcher stay focused. The research question is not simply a topic but a very particular, answerable, and measurable question.
>
> The approach to answering the research problem will depend on the specifics of the research question. Is the question more historical? Then primary textual analysis might supply an answer to the question. For instance, one research problem might be: what does the Jewish tradition state about men's dress codes? Analyzing Hebrew texts and some commentary on these issues might supply answers.
>
> Let's take another example: let's assume the reader is interested in food practices within a religious community. Food and religion are massive topics and too broad for a research project.

More narrowly, the reader is interested in gender roles in preparing food for an Easter meal within a Christian community. Specificity begins to narrow the research problem. Don't think of the problem here as an unwelcome situation but rather as an inquiry.

To formulate a research question then the reader might use this formula:

- **I am studying** food preparation within a Christian community **in order to find out** why women tend to be responsible for cooking and serving within the religious community **in order to help others understand** gender roles and food preparation within some forms of Christianity.
- Thus, my research question is: *How do gender roles determine who prepares and serves food during Christian holy days?*

For this project, the reader needs to determine what the best approach to answer this question is. Textual and historical analyses could offer responses. This question might also be appropriate for an interviewing method. However, the researcher would then need to decide who to interview. A male pastor or layperson might offer a different perspective than a female minister or religious community member. Either would supply an interesting perspective on the topic though. Another approach might be to survey congregations across a region to see how often women prepare the holy day meals. Again, which methodology is adopted will depend on what exactly needs to be determined.

Let's look at one more example together pertaining to religions and sports! A curious reader notices that at local basketball games, a religious leader guides players in prayer before and after the game (this is initial evidence). The student is interested in this topic because they are a basketball fan and are curious about religion's presence on basketball courts.

To complete the research question formula, the student might fill in the necessary information like:

- **I am studying** prayer at high school basketball games
- **in order to find out** what is being said and what is being prayed for
- **in order to help my audience understand** the role of chaplains in sports.

- The Research Question then might be: **What is the role of chaplains for local high school basketball teams pregame and post-game?**

Now, take a few minutes to construct a research question following the model provided. As a reminder, the research question formula looks like:
Research Question formula:

- **I am studying** [blank]
- **in order to find out** [blank]
- **in order to help my audience understand** [blank].
- **Research Question is:** [a question that connects these parts together]

Once you create a research question, ask yourself, what is the best method to answer this question? Is the research problem measurable? Is this a quantitative or qualitative study? What resources might be needed to address the question fully? Be sure to consider if the project's scope is too broad or narrow and if the question might require modification to form a better project direction. Take confidence in knowing that this is a process and will need refinement. So don't give up on your first try.

WHAT ARE RELIGIONS AND WHAT ARE SPORTS?

As mentioned, scholars within religious studies seriously debated (and continue to debate) what constitutes religion, religiosity, or being religious. For some, this might seem like an absurd question with a simple answer: *religion is belief in a god or deity*. There are issues with this simple assessment, however.

First, this definition of religion depends on an internal aspect of religion – belief. How do we as researchers assess what people truly believe or how much they believe? One way is to ask people if they believe in a god. Quantitative studies do just this. But whether people actually believe in a god is more complex. In the United States, according to a Pew Research Center study, about 8 out of 10 Americans believe in a god (Pew

Research Center 2017). Western Europeans have a much lower overall belief in a god, with only about 38% stating they believe in a god (O'Reilly 2018). What's terrific about some of these studies is that they dive further into the question and ask what kind of a god people believe in. Most believe in a higher power or spiritual force, and there is little consistency in what people think about the god in which they believe. Furthermore, it is a group attribution error to think that people from similar regions or areas think alike. Ultimately, belief in a god is a surface-level way of approaching religion measurements.

Second, I hope you noticed that I purposefully used belief in god and not gods. People who believe in a single deity are called monotheists and often fall into the Abrahamic religious traditions of Judaism, Christianity, and Islam. As Christianity and Islam have the largest number of adherents across the globe, some people assume a monotheistic stance on belief. Exposure effect creates this assumption, where individuals think, in this case, religion is belief in a single god because they are exposed primarily to the religious ideas of the Abrahamic traditions. Religious traditions like Hinduism incorporate millions of gods and goddesses, but like all religious traditions, there is a wide variety of perspectives on this issue. Thus, the statement that religion is belief in god is already showing monotheistic biases.

Third, questions regarding god or gods and belief in those gods fall into theological discussions. Theology is the study of god (*theos*) and theologians are trained in this study. Within theology, there are questions about the nature of deities, what information that deity has supplied to humans, and what this means for human life. Although theological studies are fascinating, these questions typically fall outside of religious studies' parameters. Remember, religious studies focuses on measurable research inquiries or problems. Religious studies is interested in how religious people (some who might believe in a god or gods) live life and the various roles of religion in societies, while theology is interested often in prescribing how people ought to live their lives based on divine revelations or textual understandings.

Then, what is religion if not belief in a deity or deities? This question has been heavily debated within the field of religious studies for decades now. As previously noted, the earliest scholars of religious studies typically applied a Western Christian definition to this question as they searched the globe for religion. This means that the earliest scholars were looking for ritual worship of gods, what, if any, dogmas and creeds existed in societies, and the origins of religion. In fact, many of the earliest scholars assumed that as Europeans, they were the most evolved people on the planet. This led them to think that if they studied religion in other parts of the world (primarily studying indigenous African and North and South American peoples), they were looking back into history. Their studies assumed the people they negatively labeled as tribal or savage were less advanced; thus, whatever religion these people practiced must be a precursor to the eventual formation of Christianity. In sum, the earliest attempts to define religion were products of Western colonial expansion.

The result of this colonial search for religion produces "religion" as a category across the globe. This might seem odd considering most people are now familiar with the categories of "world religions," but societies and regions across the globe simply do not have a concept of religion like Western colonialists carried with them. In fact, the concept of "world religions" is problematic. Tomoko Masuzawa (2005) explains that, in short, Western colonizers were part of a project to religionize the world. They sought to find religion, and their biases led them to discover what they sought. Let me provide one quick, over-simplistic example. When the British colonized India in the mid-19th century, they collected census data and established laws about religion. In one law, the 1955 Hindu Marriage Act, Hindu was an encompassing category "including not only all Buddhists, Jains, and Sikhs but also anyone who is not a Muslim, a Christian, a Parsee or a Jew" (King 1999, p. 99). The British colonizers projected a specific religious category of Hindu upon millions of people, assuming that those people must be religiously similar. Colonizers utilized religion, as a political and social category, as a tool to categorize, marginalize, and oppress populations.

Slowly scholars of religion started to come to terms with the historical biases in these definitional matters. As archival work revealed the colonial history and legacy of the term religion, scholars of religion began to adopt other ways of approaching religion. Some scholars began moving away from the notion that religions are primarily belief systems. For instance, Ninian Smart (1998) argued that religion could be understood best by its constitution. Smart posited that religion contains seven dimensions: narrative/mythological, doctrinal, ethical, institutional, material, ritual, and experiential. Smart's efforts stitch together religions' elements, how these elements form a particular cultural phenomenon, and the complexity of religions beyond creedal or doctrinal statements to which members must adhere. With these elements identified, Smart provides a litmus test for what should pass as religion. Clifford Geertz (1993) took the field in a different direction with his focus on the symbolic nature of religion. According to Geertz, religion is:

> [1] a system of symbols which acts to [2] establish powerful, pervasive, and long-lasting moods and motivations in men by [3] formulating conceptions of a general order of existence and [4] clothing these conceptions with such an aura of factuality that [5] the moods and motivations seem uniquely realistic.

Geertz's take on religion pushed scholars to consider how humans construct sets of symbols and the power these symbolic structures have on the human psyche, society, and emotional responses. Furthermore, the symbolic turn espoused by Geertz sets beliefs as secondary to a prevailing system compelling humans to act, feel, and live. These two approaches are just the tip of a massive iceberg. There are hundreds of attempts to define religion within the field. Other books provide a much richer exploration of this academic history. If interested, I recommend beginning with James Bielo's (2015) *Anthropology of Religion* in the Routledge "The Basics" series, which supplies a much more detailed examination and more examples of attempts to define religion. The debate continues with some arguing that religion as a category should not be utilized because of historical projection. Yet, even knowing the colonial project of religionization, religion is a term, concept, and category permeating the globe today.

Scholars of religion continue to debate what religion is and if religion is different from other cultural phenomena. Whereas the concept of "religion" carries with it historical baggage, the conversations surrounding what exactly defines sport centers more about what falls within the parameters of the category of sport. As my colleague and philosopher, Shawn Klein (2016) notes adeptly, as soon as "someone suggests a definition of sport: sport is X...someone else points to a kind of X that doesn't seem to be a sport" (p. xiii). Is bocce ball a sport or simply a game people play? Is video game playing a sport or, again, simply a game people play? Is there a difference? Some scholars, like historian Wray Vamplew (2021), note that what is considered as sport changes in cultures and through history. The boundaries of what constitute sports are porous, dynamic, and defined by the societies and cultures who participate and spectate.

More evident within scholarship are the values embedded in and attributed to sports participation in cultures across the globe. Sports contribute both positively and negatively to individual health and society. Most people would not question the positive effects gained through playing sports. Increased cardiovascular health along with numerous other physical and mental health benefits are assumed. Most education systems embed sports within daily school routines knowing youth need to expend energy and develop socially on playgrounds and pitches. However, sports carry the potentiality to do damage as well. From career ending injuries to youth pressures to win and compete, sports participation can be perceived as negative by some. Also, in some instances, fans are so fully invested in their team's victory that any defeat can lead to mob-like responses (Lewis 2007). Overall, sports are what people make them and tend to reflect "culture in many ways, good and bad" (Ellis 2014, p. 81). Like religion, scholars work to elucidate aspects of sports rather than strictly define what constitutes sports.

This exposes a general problem with definitions. Once a definition is constructed, there will inevitably be debated aspects, elements, or phenomena that may or may not be included within that definition. One remedy to this situation is to discuss religions and sports, plural. This is a small gesture toward recognizing a plurality of definitions and understandings of these two phenomena while also embracing the reality of the colonial influence on these topics. How we define religion ultimately matters intently in legal and political situations; however, our approach will not be to draw rigid lines about what constitutes religions. Instead, we'll draw upon several existing theories and definitions of religions. Likewise, sports, plural, is a way to indicate the variety of games people play while not being burdened by having to draw definitive lines of whether bowling, for instance, is a sport or not.

BOX 1.2 RELIGION AND SPORT IN THE NEWS

Everyday sports stories populate the news. There are sporting sections in print and digital newspapers. Journalists attempt to describe the latest statistics, trades, and wins or losses to countless fans across the globe. Online sites permit fans an opportunity to tailor their news around specific sports or teams. This allows fans to stay up-to-date with the teams they admire. Likewise, but possibly less frequently, newspapers contain stories related to religions or religious adherents. This could include religious perspectives on current political moves or stories about a local religious community.

Some of these news stories are terrific places to analyze how religion and sports are being tacitly defined. Think about it: most news stories do not take the time to define religion in the stories they are reporting. This circles back to the idea that people simply recognize religion when they see it. Similarly, there tends to be little debate about what makes the sporting section – if it's recognized as sports then it fits in the sporting category.

Is this necessarily accurate however?

Some of the stories, particularly as they center around political debates, create an opportunity to analyze how religion gets defined. For instance, as I write this chapter there is a debate about a football coach in Washington state in the United States who prays with his team on a football field at a public high school. This case went to the American Supreme Court to decide if this act was permissible within the bounds of the Constitution and if the coach was acting as a representative of the state. If the coach is a representative of the state, then potentially his actions violate the separation of church and state. However, if the prayer is understood as a personal practice and the coach, in this instance, is not a representative of the state, then the prayer could be deemed legal. The Supreme Court ruled in favor of the latter position.

Furthermore, several newspapers in the United States are focused on emerging sports like pickleball (discussed further in Chapters 4 and 6). Although this game is highlighted in the sports and culture sections, no one seems to question whether pickleball is a sport or not. The game itself is a combination of tennis, ping pong, and badminton. As pickleball is a combination of other games and not an original game in its own merit, does this disqualify the game of pickleball as a sport?

As an exercise, take some time to explore national and local news sources to examine how religions and sports are discussed, described, and presented. Who is reporting on the story? What's the perspective on sports or religions? Is religion defined as a personal, internal belief system or something else? Are sports just team sports or are individual sports included as well within the article? Which sports and which religions get the most attention in the news sources? Maybe even take a couple of articles and compare their analyses regarding religions and sports? What does this comparison reveal?

THE APPROACH OF THIS BOOK

Within this book, we'll adopt a relational approach to better understanding religions and sports. Bruce David Forbes and Jeffrey H. Mahan (2017) adopt a four-pronged relational approach to analyzing popular culture and religion in their book *Religion and Popular Culture in America*. Religion and popular culture are two cultural phenomena within the contemporary world with engaged followers, media exposure, and financial investments. These two aspects of culture often represent some of the deepest commitments of humans across the globe. Forbes and Mahan establish four relational frameworks: religion in popular culture, popular culture in religion, popular culture as religion, and religion and popular culture in dialogue. This relational analysis allows each phenomenon to exist on its own terms while also considering how they might overlap. Using these categorical frameworks, Forbes and Mahan's work opens up ways for students and scholars of the two phenomena to better understand how popular culture and religion intersect and interact. Applying Forbes and Mahan's framework more specifically to the relational aspects of religions and sports, an ever-growing element of popular culture, creates a framework for understanding key aspects of religions and sports today.

In this chapter, we began with an illustration regarding some football fans performing a ritual at a memorial site as an attempt to increase the fortunes of their team. Braving the cold conditions, the fans demonstrated their commitment to their team in a unique way on religious grounds. Thinking categorically through Forbes and Mahan's framework, we can easily observe sports in a religious space. The historical church property still conducts religious ceremonies like weddings and many consider gravesites sacred. Thus, bringing sports fandom into this space for sports reasons is sports in religion. Yet this illustration also complicates the four perspectives. Maybe we also can understand religious expressions within sports in this example? The superstitious ritual certainly seems religious in nature: Sunday morning practices on game day attempting to influence the outcome of the game. Could we ultimately make the grand move of arguing that this episode simply shows how sports are inherently religious or is this sports and religions in conversation about the importance of Poe, the city's poet? Forbes and Mahan admit the categories are not mutually exclusive and "might be better seen as interactive" (p. 21). Keep in mind the overlapping of the relational frameworks when reading the following chapters. I have adopted Forbes and Mahan's approach for the main portion of this book plus one more framework I think specifically applies to competition between religions and sports.

Possibly the most obvious chapter within the book due to its highly visible nature is the following chapter on religious expressions in sports. This chapter examines ways that religious elements find their way into sporting fields, courts, and pitches.

Initially looking at the way that athletes bring their religious expressions into their competitive arenas, this chapter examines the questions around whether religion should be brought into sports. Although there are some athletes championed as people of faith by publicly displaying their religiosity, other athletes might feel more vulnerable when it comes to religious expressions. This leads to questions around benefits from publicly displaying religiosity on the competitive field. Are there economic benefits? Why would some players choose not to display their religiosity? Furthermore, this chapter examines less visible case studies like specific examples of Muslim professional athletes fasting during Ramadan and debates over female Muslim athletes' attire and how this affects athletic performance. Overall, this chapter complicates the notion of religion in sports and looks at how secular perspectives shape responses.

Less publicly visible are the ways that some religious communities adopt sports and play as a means to further their objectives. Chapter 3, "Sports in Religions," investigates how religious leaders and innovators utilize competitive sports as a means of disciplining, proselytizing, and expanding their social relevance. Looking initially at team sports, this chapter highlights examples of Christian communities embedding "sports ministries" into their practices. Moving the conversation from "muscular Christianity," the idea that American Christians used sports as a means to counter the supposed feminization of Christian men, this chapter shows that sports are an innovative way of embedding religious ideals, sharing doctrines, and inviting outsiders into the religious fold. While some adopt sports as a means of proselytizing, other religious groups employ sports as a means of socially integrating. This chapter studies how some Jewish adherents found some social acceptance through participating in certain sports like boxing, swimming, and golf. Analyzing proselytizing and integration attempts together reveal the power dynamics inherent in societies and how religion and sports operate within those dynamics.

Once the scaffolding is in place for understanding religions and sports, the fourth chapter examines theoretical arguments for how sports mirror, or are inherently, religious devotion. This content challenges the notion that sports and religions are categorically distinct; instead, the argument is that sports and religions are functionally the same. Looking specifically at the argument that people are disenchanted in the modern world, the fourth chapter highlights sports as a religious-like means of re-enchantment. Focusing specifically on an emerging sport called pickleball, collected evidence demonstrates the religious-like devotion to a younger sport today. Continuing, this chapter offers two counters to the "sports as religions" argument. The first involves inverting the "sports as religions" arguments and questioning whether religions are a form of play. The second involves a critique of the "sports as religions" position, questioning the colonial legacy embedded in the argument.

Focusing particularly on professional basketball, Chapter 5, "Religions and Sports in Dialogue," examines the discourse between religious ideas and leaders and professional athletes. Specifically, there are two examples utilized in this section of the book. The chapter begins by acknowledging the inequalities and imperfections within sports. Following this, we examine the Papal invitation to NBA players to discuss race relations globally and the Black Lives Matter movement in the United States. Next, we consider the case of a professional basketball player who revealed his homosexuality and the social media response to his coming out. Both of these examples demonstrate that sports and religiosity are often communicating, sharing ideas, and informing the other phenomenon. Furthermore, a key aspect of athletes across the globe today is the engagement of social justice issues within arenas, fields, and courts. As more professional athletes utilize their platform to speak out against racial injustices, gun violence, and gender inequality the question must be asked, are athletes the priests and prophets of the contemporary world? As people disaffiliate with traditional religion, some look for voices that challenge social inequalities, and, for many, athletes are the primary voice offering a critique of negative societal norms in public spheres. Specifically highlighted in this chapter are racial injustices and sexuality and how athletes have utilized their platforms to advance equality on these issues. This chapter asks if athletes and coaches are displacing religious leaders as the moral compass of societies around the globe, and how sporting spaces become public spaces for political discourse. Ultimately, the material in this chapter demonstrates how all the relational angles of religions and sports can be simultaneously active.

Adding to Forbes and Mahan's frameworks, Chapter 6 "Religions and Sports in Competition" explores how these two cultural phenomena are vying for members' investments and time. After introducing the idea of a cultural marketplace, the chapter examines how skateboarding could be a spiritual exercise, competing with traditional forms of religion and spirituality. This example shows how qualitative studies help elucidate research questions regarding people's perspectives of their activities. Then we examine a quantitative study analyzing the devotion of individuals to the game of pickleball compared to religious or spiritual commitments. These two cases offer qualitative and quantitative examples of how research can be conducted to gain deeper understandings of the relationships between religions and sports. Overall, this chapter offers a foundation for the reader to consider how they might enter into research related to religions and sports.

Finally, the last chapter examines sports and religions during the COVID-19 global pandemic. During this epidemic, numerous countries suspended religious meetings and sporting events as a means of mitigating the spread of the virus. The isolation of the pandemic had many religious people longing for their religious community, and likewise, many sports fans longing for their sports to restart. Using the suspension of play and the minimizing of religious meetings during the pandemic, this chapter shows how important these two phenomena are in the modern world. Readers will understand that sports and religions as an "opiate of the masses," which is generally viewed as a denunciation of religion, could be understood as a positive, and how live sports and religious gatherings resonate differently for people compared to virtual meetings or replays of sporting events. Ending the book by thinking about the absence of religions and sports pushes us to consider the temporality of human phenomena. Sports and religions evolve with human historical advancements and are dynamic in nature.

BOX 1.3 INSIDER/OUTSIDER DYNAMICS

The love of religions or sports brings many scholars to research these phenomena. For instance, a Manchester United soccer fan might be compelled to conduct research on the topic of the soccer team's fans and history. However, this raises a potential dilemma: can a fan of a particular team who is devoted to that team conduct unbiased research about that team? Similarly, if a person is an adherent to specific religious tradition (i.e. Hinduism, Judaism, Islam, etc.), can that person objectively study the religious tradition of which they are a part?

This is a question considered in religious studies. The basis of the question is can an insider study X from the inside? The complementary question is can an outsider research X from the outside. There are good arguments for and against each. For instance, an insider already has access to specific terminologies and languages used within some religious traditions, like if a Muslim spoke of *ummah*, a scholar who happens to be Muslim will typically already know that the term refers to the Muslim community. A non-Muslim would need to investigate this term to familiarize themselves with the specifics of this term. However, an outsider might recognize key aspects to a ritual that might be so familiar to an insider that the familiarity renders it quite invisible. An example of this is when a practice is so common an insider might not even think to question it.

This insider/outsider scholarly dynamic shows that there is very little we can do about our positionality to the project. What we can do is admit our position and then work to, as much as possible, bracket our feelings, thoughts, and emotions about the project. So, the Manchester United fan would need to admit their commitments and devotions and how this could interfere with their research analysis and conclusions. Furthermore, they would need to work intently to not let their fandom interfere with their scholarly explorations.

This is a dilemma we all potentially face in any research project. Research is not neutral even though we would like to think that it is. Every scholar in every field must reflectively consider their positionality as they approach their research. An economics scholar who thinks capitalism is the best economic system must cordon off that opinion as they conduct research comparing capitalism and socialism, for instance. Ideally, when conducting research, the final data and its conclusions are what they are, whether we personally agree or not.

Now is a good time for the reader to reflect on why and how they come to the study of religions and sports. Does the reader have sporting or religious commitments that could potentially sway their opinions on specific research? If so, what are these? What are your motivations in better understanding the relationship between religions and sports? Have you already determined in your mind what the relationship of religions and sports is? If so, how can you bracket this to be more open-minded as you work through the various perspectives in this book? How do you come to the topic of religions and sports? Are you a skeptic or a believer in the relationship at this moment? If so, why? What experience formed these vantage points?

CHAPTER SYNOPSIS

The study of religions and sports has a long history of analysis. We are fortunate at this time to be able to build from the previous research and theorizing conducted by researchers. This creates a wealth of knowledge in which we can engage and supplies us a starting point for understanding the relationships between religions and sports. Additionally, religious studies' multidisciplinary approach can help examine various angles to the question about the relationships between religions and sports. In short, religious studies as a disciplinary field creates a toolbox of resources, approaches, and techniques for studying sports and religions' relationships, intersections, and overlaps.

We noted briefly the self-reflective movement within the field of religious studies acknowledging how previous theories were undergirded with Western, colonial assumptions about religion. This is important to keep in mind when considering the history of the field but also so that we can try to avoid similar mistakes in our examinations. Religions and sports, in the plural, offer a simplistic way of denoting the broad-scale variety within each of the cultural phenomena. Throughout this book, we will use multiple case studies as illustrations for our claims. Certainly, debates will arise about how specific examples fit into the religions and sports categories. This is fine. Good academic debate is part of the knowledge-building processes.

Ultimately, this book surveys the relationships between religions and sports in an introductory fashion. The goal is less about settling long standing debates within specific disciplinary fields and more so about introducing the reader to these conversations around our topic, supplemented with numerous case studies. Remember to be generous to your conversation partners and charitable with your positions.

RECOMMENDED READING

There are numerous books dealing with the expansive history of the study of religion. Each of these books mines through academic history to expose weaknesses and strengths of past studies and their continuing contribution to the field of religious studies. In addition to Masuzawa's *The Invention of World Religions* (2005), Daniel Dubuisson's *The Western Construction of Religion* (2003) supplies a rich historical account of how we get to where "World Religions" and religion are normalized in Western societies and around the globe today. Both books dive deep into the colonial roots of religions and the academic study of religion. For a good analysis of the evolution of the term "religion," I recommend Brent Nongbri's *Before Religion* (2013). Nongbri's work demonstrates the Western history of religion as a term and how this term evolved. *Nine Theories of Religion* (2014), by Daniel Pals, provides students of religious studies with summaries of the important early thinkers considering how to approach religion. Pals focuses his attention on the Western canon of intellectual thinkers and how interests in studying religion outside of theology matured.

Likewise, scholarship provides ample analyses of sports and sports cultures. For an historical survey of the development of sports, I recommend *Sports: The First Five Millennia* by Allen Guttman (2004). Pertaining to the importance and value of sports, I recommend Wray Vamplew's *Games People Played* (2001) and *Consuming Sports* (2004) by Garry Crawford. The former looks at the history of particular sports and the importance of play. The latter discusses how fandoms emerge and what life is like for those devoted to particular teams. Shawn Klein's volume *Defining Sport* (2016) is a collection of essays grappling with several case studies, ideas, and theories regarding what sport is. Like religions, entire cultures are built around sports; Tony Schirato's *Understanding Sports Culture* (2007) shows the complexity of sport industries in the contemporary world. Finally, Stephen Mumford's *A Philosopher Looks at Sport* (2021) examines, simply put, why sports matter.

RELIGIONS IN SPORTS

In the first chapter, we established the complexities that surround defining religion and demonstrated how religious studies, as an academic field, could assist in analyzing religions and sports both quantitatively and qualitatively. The tools available in the discipline of religious studies establish several means of approaching specific case studies including psychological, historical, sociological, anthropological, and philosophical approaches. Studying religions and sports opens up significant pathways to understanding humans and their activities better. The two cultural phenomena of religions and sports are held dearly by people around the globe. Being a member of a religious tradition and/or a sports fan brings with it certain privileges, prestige, and, often, enters one into a community of similarly-committed individuals. These two spaces of social activity share – often intense – practices, loyalties, and identities for people. Studying these practices, loyalties, and identities are central to religious studies.

Having adopted Forbes and Mahan's frameworks for the bulk of this book, in this chapter we look more closely at *religions in sports*. In order to properly explore this relationship, we will begin by thinking about how we typically think. Processing our daily lives and the world in which we dwell requires us to create categorical divisions in order to determine what something is and is not. After looking at categories, concepts, and spaces, we will look at the ways that religious expressions find their way into sporting spaces, primarily through focusing our attention on religious expressions of individual athletes. To some this is

DOI: 10.4324/9781003362630-2

obvious because religious expressions appear frequently in some sports. To others, this will read as quite foreign. Looking more closely at religious expressions shows how some conflicts could emerge for athletes and teams. We will focus much of our attention on Muslim athletes and how Islamic religious commitments find their way into sporting spaces.

CATEGORIES, CONCEPTS, AND SPACES

If I say the word "sport" what springs into your mind? Many of us think less about the universal notion of sport and more about specificities we have experienced or knowledge we have gained. For some an image of a specific sport springs to mind. Globally soccer (or football) is the most played and watched sport so there's a good chance an image of a soccer ball, field, or stadium emerged. Others might visualize an element or aspect related to basketball, American football, lacrosse, rugby, or hockey. There are numerous different sporting options. These thoughts could be related to a specific sport played by the individual, the one in which the individual invests their fan commitments, or sheer exposure to a particular sport. Some might think even more specifically about a particular team. This could be a team on which one has played or a team that captures the imagination of the individual. Being a team fan is a significant aspect of life for many people around the globe, and the commitment to that team can take precedence over thoughts about different sports. Drilling down further into our thoughts, an individual athlete could be the first image appearing in one's mind when considering sports. Athletes like Michael Jordan, Serena Williams, or Pelé evoke strong reactions from some fans who spend time debating who is the greatest of all time within specific sports. In fact, the image of these athletes, for some devoted fans, represents the sport itself. There are different images that an individual could think of when they contemplate sports, due to the ubiquitous nature of sports around the globe. More images conjured could be of team logos or mascots, or a historic sporting moment could be replayed in the mind. The list could go on and on.

If we conducted a similar thought experiment around the term "religion" we would also see an infinite number of potential thoughts. An individual's thoughts might hone in on one religious tradition. This could include images of the Buddha or a monk, a Christian crucifix or cross, or a Hindu deity or practitioner. Thousands of images and symbols permeate religious traditions forming a trove of different ideas, practices, or rituals. Funerals, weddings, and various rites of passage could spring to mind. Thinking less about one religion and more about a specific religious belief or practice in which an individual is more familiar is common. Like sports, a specific religious experience could be recalled. An impactful religious occurrence, whether positive or negative, can be imprinted and be part of the brain's quick recall activity. Or a person who exemplifies a religious tradition could surface. This might be someone who is highly respected by the thinker and tremendous respect for this person might exist. Yet another direction could be a particularly sacred place, such as a temple, mosque, or another religiously-associated building. Others might recall a text or scripture that is particularly meaningful for them. Again, there are millions of possibilities within this exercise.

This exercise illustrates two things: we all think in a similar fashion with universals but uniquely with specifics. Universals denote the shared broad categories and concepts like sports and religions, but also government, economics, or language; specifics take the universal category and find particulars like specific kinds of economic systems: traditional, command, market, and mixed economies. Our thought processes rely on employing broad categories. These categories permit humans to move quickly through our thoughts by compartmentalizing concepts. We tend to separate religions from sports from politics, etc. Doing this certainly isn't a perfect way of thinking but does allow us to rapidly process our immediate worlds. Daniel Kahneman argues that our "mental activities become fast and automatic through prolonged practice" (2011, p. 22). This automatic way of thinking establishes a means for humans to communicate through language deployment. When we speak of sports, we all tend to assume we all mean the same things. This might be inaccurate, but this is our assumption. Along with the broad universal concepts and categories, our personal experiences – education, childhood, etc. – shape our mental processes. Our brain uses these activities to formulate our associative ideas and thoughts along with our categories. In other words, we often think of specifics associated within our categories. Or we have emotional attachments that emerge during our thoughts that color our perspectives. Asking someone who has experienced religious trauma to detail their first thoughts about religion will probably evoke different responses from someone who has had a profound and impactful religious experience. In sum, universals and specifics permit quick thinking, categorizing, and communicating about objects, events, and practices in everyday life.

If we visualize this categorical way of thinking, we might simply understand religions and sports as two distinctive categories and concepts. These are two separate entities and concepts imagined in separate domains of life. Religious activity takes place in religiously-designated spaces or private spaces; sports, likewise, operate within sporting spaces like arenas, gyms, or outdoor fields. In this frame of thinking, whether recreational or professional, sports are competitive events not associated with religion. Furthermore, religions, fundamentally, are about the sacred, supernatural, or transcendent aspects of life, not sports competitions. Figure 2.1 is an oversimplified way of visualizing this distinctive way of processing religions and sports.

As Figure 2.1 indicates, religions and sports exist as two separate categories. Religions exist in our global world. These religions are composed of practices, texts, rules for life, and ways of being in the world. Likewise, sports exist in our world. These sports have their own set of rules, practices, legends, and ways of being in the world. They operate unattached and in designated places. Again, this is oversimplified but illustrative of

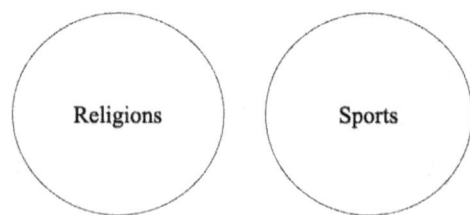

Figure 2.1

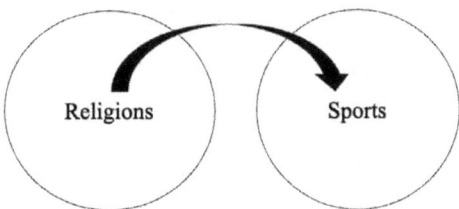

Figure 2.2

how people understand and process the world in which they dwell. Often this is demonstrated when I tell people I teach a religions and sports course at my university. The response is sometimes confusion about how these two entities could be associated at all. Why? Sports are sports, and religions are religions in people's minds.

Our thoughts carry much more complexity; yet, pushed to respond expeditiously, the majority of people might think of the relationships of religions and sports initially as such. Religions are separate and distinct from sports. It's that simple. If we think in this manner, typically with our quick-thinking reflexes, then we could imagine that sometimes religious expressions find their way into sporting spaces. This does not mean that sports and religions are the same; rather that expressions from one infiltrate the domain of the other. In this case, religious expressions work their way into sporting domains, arenas, gyms, or fields. With categorical distinctions, Figure 2.2 represents crudely the notion that religion finds its way into sports.

Typically, this does not equate to an entire religious community or organization taking over a sporting space; rather this refers to an individual athlete bringing their religiosity into a sport. Taking this approach helps us then to concentrate on episodes where the publicly-expressed religious devotion of athletes are found within the games that people play. This often looks like a single athlete or a group of athletes revealing their religious devotion before, during, or after a game. In other words, these athletes make their religious ideas visible while competing in a sport.

EXPLICIT RELIGIOUS EXPRESSIONS IN SPORTS

Scholars of several different academic disciplines identify, describe, and theorize the various religious expressions discovered in sporting spaces. Many psychologists are interested in the potential benefits for athletes in performing religious rituals before games across the globe (Dömötör et al. 2016; Brooks et al. 2016; Hagan and Schack 2019). These studies focus attention on the emotional and behavioral reasons an athlete might perform a pregame ritual. One study discovered that "superstitious acts in sports are performed to regulate one's emotions and bring the uncertain or seemingly uncontrollable events under control by switching from a negative to a positive mindset that aids the athlete in performance" (Dömötör et al. 2016, p. 369). The pregame rituals then calm the nerves and build the athlete's confidence for game performance. Concurring with this study, another study conducted by John Hagan and Thomas Schack (2017) demonstrates how localized pregame rituals in African contexts rely on songs, dance, verbalization, and prayer to embolden athletes and boost confidence. Yet, another study took this one step further and posited, "simply performing a sequence of pre-performance actions does not reduce anxiety or improve performance unless imbued with meaning" (Brooks et al. 2016, p. 82). For example, although an athlete might adopt the practice of touching their jersey number three times before a game, unless that athlete ascribes a deeper meaning to that pregame ritual then it potentially is ineffective. Whether or not pregame rituals actually aid in game performance or if the rituals operate as a placebo convincing the athlete they will improve performance matters little for our topic; rather, these studies illustrate a very small sampling of how some scholars trained in psychology approach pregame rituals for analysis. Many of the pregame rituals might be conducted off the field while others might be highly visible and include fan participation.

For viewers of sports, there are certain common religious expressions that are almost expected. A player making the sign of the cross when approaching the batter's box in baseball or a soccer player pointing to the sky after they score a goal are simple and minor gestures revealing religious devotion. In these simple moves, there are usually no words articulated; rather these are simply signifiers used to show devotion, attribute abilities, or express gratitude to a deity or supernatural entity. Yet, they are visible in a sporting space. The athlete chooses to make these religious actions. Religion finds its way into sporting spaces. Sometimes this also works behind the scenes. For example, on Sunday mornings in Chicago, a Catholic priest offers Mass for workers and players at the stadium in Wrigley Field. The priest, Father Burke Masters, who is a former athlete himself, details, "The two things that I love to combine in my ministry is faith and sports, so this was a great opportunity. And having played baseball, this couldn't get much better for me" (Duriga 2016). Religious expressions in sporting spaces sometimes get normalized with particular athletes, teams, or organizations.

In recent years, one of the most talked about religious gestures was that of NFL quarterback Tim Tebow. Tebow rose to fame while playing quarterback for the University of Florida Gators football team. During his time with the Gators, he successfully led his team to two BCS National Championships and received the Heisman Trophy award – an award recognizing the most outstanding player in college football that season. With his dual threat of running and passing abilities, Tebow tallied impressive statistics. He accounted for over 80 touchdowns (over 50 rushing touchdowns), more than 9,000 passing yards, and almost 3,000 rushing yards while leading the University of Florida to two national championships. Beyond his tremendous wins and statistics, while at the University of Florida, he also received attention because he painted bible verse references in his eye black (a grease substance used to reduce glare from the sun). These references included John 3:16, Mark 8:36, and Ephesians 2:8–10. In 2010, after his illustrious career at the University of Florida, the Denver Broncos drafted Tebow, and the following year, he became the starting quarterback. His professional career failed to match his college success, however; Tebow had a short-lived National Football League (NFL) career, spending two seasons with the Broncos and another season as a backup quarterback for the New York Jets. After his professional football career ended, Tebow turned to the sport of baseball but never made the major leagues.

Tim Tebow's fame as an athlete often centered on his religious beliefs and the ways in which he expressed that religiosity on and off the field. After a strong win against the Miami Dolphins during his professional career, Tebow knelt on one knee in prayer while fans and teammates celebrated the victory. Thus in 2011, "Tebowing" became an Internet sensation and a social trend. People from across the globe mimicked Tebow's posture, uploading photos to various blogs, social media sites, and forums. For many sharing the same faith, Tebow was seen as a courageous Christian, publicly expressing his devotion to his god. Before this, Tebow had already established himself as a person willing to engage in hot religio-political issues in the United States. During the 2010 Super Bowl, Tebow appeared with his mom in a pro-life, anti-abortion commercial for Focus on the Family, a conservative Christian organization headquartered in Colorado. As a champion of a conservative-leaning Christian faith, Tebow achieved celebrity status. Regarding Tebowing, the quarterback stated, "It's something I do that's prayer for me, and then it got hyped up as 'Tebowing.'" Tebow seemed to welcome the attention, continued Tebowing on the sidelines of games, and eventually trademarked it, arguing that he needed to control usage of his kneeling posture.

While Tim Tebow's act of devotion – kneeling in prayer – was celebrated by many, another prayer incident received a different reaction. In 2014, another NFL player celebrated a touchdown. Husain Abdullah, a safety for the Kansas City Chiefs, intercepted a pass from quarterback Tom Brady and returned the interception for a touchdown. As part of his celebration, Abdullah, who is Muslim, performed the sajdah (or Sujūd) in the endzone. This type of prayer looks slightly different than a kneeling prayer; a prostration of the body characterizes this prayer. Abdullah fell to both knees and lowered his helmet to the ground. The NFL referees, potentially confused by this posture, threw a penalty flag on Abdullah, and the Chiefs received a 15-yard unsportsmanlike conduct penalty. The NFL quickly responded the next day by condemning the penalty. Referring to his touchdown and interception, Abdullah stated, "If I got a pick, I'm going to prostrate before God in the end zone."

These two examples indicate that religious expressions in sporting spaces are quite complex and deserve more consideration. These examples of athletes publicly praying shows how organizations can respond differently. Familiarity with certain expressions establishes some practices as acceptable while others are penalized. We could ask how far does freedom extend to express one's religiosity in sporting spaces? The answer to this question will depend on the national context. In some countries, there are explicit limits to what can and cannot be conducted publicly. In other countries, like the United States, there tends to be an acceptance of minor expressions but a tacit agreement recognizing the limitations of this acceptance. For instance, if an athlete reads from a religious text during a game or uses the game as a religious or worship service most would consider those actions inappropriate. Additionally, it is easy to imagine that religious practices like animal sacrifice (as referenced in the baseball films *Bull Durham* and *Major League*) in sporting spaces would alarm fans.

The examples of Tebow and Abdullah praying during NFL games shows a difference in perception and reception. Why would Tebow, unlike other players, choose to express his religious faith publicly? Some might argue that he maintains a higher devotion. However, being rewarded, not punished, for his faith certainly creates conditions for him to continue his religious expressions. Although some might have defended Abdullah's right to prayer in the stadium, he did not receive the same level of support from football fans. Tebow was championed as a religious hero; Abdullah was cited as a victim of a simple misunderstanding. Tebow also profited financially from his overt Christianity. Tebow earned invitations to speak at churches and conferences and received a handsome stipend to deliver messages in these venues. Early in his Denver Broncos career, before even taking the field, Tebow's jersey sales were among the highest in the NFL. Most people are unfamiliar with Husain Abdullah's story.

Bringing religious expressions to sporting arenas is not limited to athletes. Some fans opt to use their religion to change the outcome of a game. Additionally, different religions can enter into a sporting site simultaneously. Consider Lyton Ncube's

(2017) study of Zimbabwean soccer. Ncube found co-existing religious rituals performed by fans on behalf of their soccer team. These include Christian, African Traditional Religion, and Rastafarian rituals of prayers, medicines, and songs, all abound within the fans' sections of the pitches. Fans tend to use whatever religious resources they have available to ward off curses, provide good luck for the team's success, and celebrate victories or explain defeats. Ncube concludes his study with this observation: "football (soccer) is a critical site for the articulation, performance, and contestation of various religious myths and rituals" (p. 85). Fans, typically less restricted by team regulations, can decide, within limits, to deploy their religiosity in order to serve their team's efforts while also considering what is socially acceptable within sporting spaces.

> ### BOX 2.1 PROFESSIONAL ATHLETE'S RELIGIOSITY
>
> In the contemporary world, professional athletes must decide how to navigate and negotiate their public relations. This navigation often includes a public relations manager and an agent who help the athlete consider their public persona. The athlete might work to promote a particular charity or nonprofit organization, demonstrating their charitable character. Sometimes athletes find themselves in a negative spotlight after a physical altercation or familial conflict is made public. These incidents often go viral, with millions of fans and trolls commenting on incidents along with media commentary. With social media and video capabilities in everyone's hands, athletes must manage the public presentation of who they are.
>
> Like other public relations issues, sometimes athletes must consider how much to share their religious ideas, spirituality, or lack of religious practices. There are several considerations regarding this issue. First, the athlete might consider where to be vocal or quiet about their religious beliefs. For some athletes, religion is a private affair conducted in separate venues outside the purview of fans and the public eye. If an athlete does reveal their religiosity, they often open themselves up to public scrutiny. Will some fans think less or more of the athlete for sharing their religious ideas publicly? Would a religious move or reference even matter to most fans who might

be more concerned with the athlete's abilities and successes on the field or court? Taking it even further, should the athlete divulge their religious stances on political issues and become involved in public debate? If so, what will this possibly do to their fanbase or teammates' opinion of them?

Some athletes take a less vocal route and maybe share their religious affiliation on a personal website or social media but rarely reference the religion otherwise. This route pronounces an affiliation without giving further details into the specifics of that personal religiosity. For example, an athlete might include Christian, Muslim, or Jewish alongside information of birthplace or school affiliation. This move leaves the interpretation of the scale of religious devotion open ended.

Others like Tim Tebow lean into their religious devotion and use it to their advantage. As religions form insider/outsider dynamics, public religiosity for an athlete could produce an instant fan base. For instance, once Tebow proclaims he is a conservative Christian, conservative Christians will take notice of Tebow as a member of their ingroup. Certainly, this isn't always the case but if done well religious affiliation can be advantageous for an athlete's marketing.

To get a better perspective on the ways athletes either opt to share or not share their religious affiliation, stances, and practices, take some time to investigate online. A good start is by simply searching for a specific athlete and religion in an Internet search engine. For example, as a child, I was a fan of the New York Mets baseball team, specifically the outfielder Darryl Strawberry. I'm not sure where my devotion to the Mets emerged, but I distinctly remember being impressed with Strawberry's left-handed batting swing. As a kid, I worked on switch hitting and taught myself how to bat left-handed like Strawberry. Upon reflection, I knew very little about Strawberry's religious affiliation. With a quick search online, I discovered Strawberry, after his professional career, has been outspoken about his Christian faith. Alongside his wife, Tracy, they publish books about faith, and Strawberry speaks publicly with other athletes about his religious commitments.

What about your favorite athlete? Is there any indication of their religiosity or spirituality? Why might this athlete choose to disclose or not disclose their religious commitments? Or pick a more creative way of randomizing players for research. For example, try conducting a fantasy sports draft with any sport. Numerous fantasy sports leagues are available for free with ESPN and the like. Once a team is drafted, including players from several positions, conduct research regarding the religious affiliations of the starters of the fantasy team. Once you complete the research, question whether there are any variables correlating with more or less obvious religiosity. Are there certain positions in which players tend to be more religious? If so, why? Additionally, if there is a larger pool of researchers, try drafting fantasy teams from multiple sports and then conduct the religiosity research. Are there certain sports that tend to consist of players who are more religiously devout? For instance, if a game is more violent, are the players more likely to reveal their religious identity?

ISLAMIC EXPRESSIONS IN SPORTS

The examples of Husain Abdullah and Tim Tebow are highly obvious and overt. Fans can see the expressions, and the players perform their religious expressions on the fields of play. There are certainly other obvious and visible expressions to consider. Some players are quite vocally outspoken about their religiosity. Consider Muhammad Ali, the legendary boxer, who converted to the Nation of Islam in 1964, the more mainstream Sunni branch of Islam in 1975, and then embraced Sufi mystical practices later in life. In his interviews, Ali acknowledged his devotion to Islam. After defeating Joe Frazier in Zaire, Ali boldly stated, "I proved that Allah is God. Elijah Muhammad is the messenger and I have faith in them." Elijah Muhammad was the founder of the Nation of Islam and profoundly influential in Ali's initial conversion to Islam. When questioned further as to whether the victory was the greatest moment of Ali's life, Ali rejected this sentiment and instead proclaimed that the greatest moment of his life was "when I met Elijah Muhammed, the freedom speaker to black people." Ali's religiosity knew no bounds, and he articulated his faith in and out of the boxing ring.

Although Ali vocalized his Muslim faith openly, other Islamic practices performed by some Muslim athletes are less overt and visible, and the reception is quite mixed by media and society. Retired NBA basketball champion Hakeem Olajuwon's religious practices demonstrate this. Hakeem "the Dream" is a Nigerian-born basketball player who played the majority of his professional career with the Houston Rockets. Olajuwon was known for his spectacular footwork and his ability to maneuver around the basket. For a seven-foot (2.13 meters) center in the NBA, Olajuwon tended to be much quicker than his defender, using his "dream shake" to freeze his opponents. His career accomplishments include two NBA world championships, MVP of both of those series, two-time NBA defensive player of the year, an Olympic gold medalist in 1996, and many more achievements.

At an early stage in his basketball career, Olajuwon became a more devout Muslim, altering his name's spelling from Akeem to Hakeem, which is closer to the Arabic spelling. During this time, Olajuwon describes, "I studied the Qur'an every day. At home, at the mosque...I was soaking up the faith and learning new meanings each time I turned a page" (Olajuwon and Knobler 1996). Beginning in 1995, Olajuwon decided to participate in fasting during the Islamic holy month of Ramadan. During this holy month, Muslims practice self-restraint and abstain from eating and drinking, as well as other practices like sexual activity, between dawn and dusk each day. After the sun sets, Muslims typically gather for a meal and prayers. For athletes who require healthy caloric intake and hydration, fasting might seem like a dangerous practice. Playing at the professional level depletes the human body and drains it of nutritional resources, but Olajuwon devoted himself to fasting even during the NBA season. In fact, Olajuwon argues his abilities increased during a fast: "I feel much better. I feel lighter, faster, much more mentally focused" (Kilpatrick 2022). While fasting, Olajuwon often accomplished extraordinary statistical achievements. His performances often excelled during Ramadan. However, his teammate, Robert Horry, saw the complications of fasting: "I always felt bad for him. I don't mean for that to come across wrong, but when you are playing an NBA game, you got to have massive reserves of energy" (Young 2022).

Olajuwon would become a role model for Muslim athletes, even advising other Muslim NBA players like Enes Kanter.

While the media often praised Olajuwon for his religious devotion, Olajuwon wasn't the only Muslim player in the NBA during his career. At the same time that Hakeem Olajuwon played in the NBA, Mahmoud Abdul-Rauf, who played for the Denver Nuggets, gained notoriety for another religiously-inspired move. Specifically, Abdul-Rauf decided not to stand during the national anthem beginning in the 1995–96 basketball season. Born Chris Jackson in Gulfport, Mississippi, he converted to Islam in 1991 and changed his name. Abdul-Rauf cited his Islamic faith in deciding not to stand during the national anthem. The NBA responded by suspending Abdul-Rauf, arguing that NBA rules specified that all players must stand during the anthem. His refusal to stand during the national anthem "received criticism from Olajuwon for not knowing proper Islam," as well as from some radio and television commentators (Mwaniki 2019, p. 223). He "received many letters, including death threats and suggestions he 'go back to Africa'" (Alpert 2015, p. 130). After the season, the Nuggets traded Abdul-Rauf to the Sacramento Kings, and his decision not to stand for the "Star Spangled Banner" forever tainted his career.

As in the case of Abdul-Rauf, sometimes sports organizations (i.e., the National Basketball Association) interject their decision-making abilities to counter that of specific players' actions. As it pertains to standing or not standing for the national anthem, the NBA limited Abdul-Rauf's freedom of expression and backed its rule that players must stand for the anthem. These organizations must weigh the interests and reputation of the league against individual players' rights. Olajuwon's decision to fast and the generally positive reception from fans and media brought useful attention to the player and, thus, to the league. The NBA, as an organization, could set Olajuwon as an example of the religious devotion of its basketball players. Abdul-Rauf's case would re-emerge in later years as other players refused to stand in the NFL, NBA, and soccer leagues. The leagues would then consider the situation in the broader political context, fans' support, and the sheer number of players joining in. The leagues must also look at the financial consequences of the player's actions. Tebow's jersey sales and notoriety certainly influenced the decision to permit Tebowing on the football field. In sum, there are several considerations for athletes, their teams, and the leagues they play in as it relates to religious expressions within sporting spaces.

In all of these cases, religion found its way into the public careers of particular athletes, and, hence, into sporting spaces. Like Ali, Olajuwon and Abdul-Rauf were open and honest about their Islamic devotion. The responses to their religiously-inspired practices were drastically different. The media depicted and perceived Olajuwon's practices as an individual, religious choice with little to no effect on anyone except Olajuwon. Potentially, had Olajuwon's basketball performances suffered from his fasting, fans might have criticized his religious decisions due to ranking the team's success over his individual religious practices. Abdul-Rauf's religious devotion was understood as unpatriotic and un-American. His career suffered and threats were received because of his decisions. His practices were perceived and depicted as against the rules and antagonistic against American society as a whole. In sum, Olajuwon was depicted as a reasonable Muslim "amenable to American society," while Abdul-Rauf was portrayed as a "bad" Muslim (Mwaniki 2019, p. 223). These two cases illustrate how religion encroaches into sporting spaces, and opposite responses emerge from these occurrences.

BOX 2.2 RELIGIOUS UNIFORMS/SPORTS UNIFORMS

As sports and religions are often performed by collective groups of people, there typically exists some type of uniformity of its members. In some instances, beliefs, values, or perspectives are central to the uniformity. For religions, many groups' coherence depends on members adhering or, at least, assenting to common values and perspectives. Sports exist similarly. Team members must maintain the idea of winning a championship, trophy, or medal, or, minimally, that individual members are committed to the team's success. This obviously varies in different sports and religions.

Beliefs, values, and perspectives are internal ideas. In order to show team or religious coherence, dress codes visibly display a uniformity of members. Shared color schemes or types of clothing show who is in the ingroup. Teams and leagues require uniformity of sportswear for safety, to ease the job of referees, and for marketing purposes. In most sports, teams share a design or emblem, creating a communal element. Think of your favorite team. What do the uniforms look like? Furthermore, fans often indicate their allegiances by wearing replicas of their favorite team's jersey, shirt, or gear. Jerseys might display a favorite player's name or a specific number of a player. Minimally, many fans will wear their team's colors. Thus, there exists a uniformity between the team and its fans.

Some religious traditions also prescribe a uniform type of dress, although this drastically varies. Some traditions might require specific types of dress during religious gatherings, while some might require everyday uniformity. Some dress codes are attempts to stay within the bounds of moral foundations. For example, a religious man might only wear long pants covering the entire waist and legs to the ankles whenever they leave their home. Or a prayer shawl could be required whenever a religious person prays. In some cases, a vague homogeneity permeates a religious group's dress. All the men might wear a suit coat and tie along with slacks, but the colors, fabrics, etc., could vary.

Within Islam there exists a diversity of dress code requirements for women. Some Muslim women are required to conceal their entire bodies by wearing a burqa. This type of covering typically only has a small mesh veil for the woman to see through. This is prescribed for complete modesty for women who are in public. More commonly Muslim women wear a hijab. The hijab is a headscarf typically covering the head and neck area but leaves the face open. Hijabs range in colors and fabric materials.

Pertaining to religions in sports, one can imagine a potential conflict between sporting and religious uniforms. If both are required by members as a means of designating membership, small deviations can make a player stand out among teammates. The hijab is an example in contemporary society where sporting and religious uniforms sometimes clash. Ibtihaj Muhammed, a fencer on the American Olympic team, contended with this issue. In 2016, Muhammed won a bronze medal (and was the first Muslim American to do so) when competing in fencing while wearing a hijab. According to Muhammed, she chose fencing because the sport already requires the competing athletes' bodies to be fully covered. Muhammed chose her hijab to match the rest of her uniform. Although she was successful in her career, Muhammed claims she suffered discrimination from her coaches and teammates and received death threats while competing (Deb 2018). Based on her experiences, she opened her own line of fashionable and sporting hijabs. When interviewed, she stated, "Every woman should have the choice to wear what she wants and the opportunity to play sport, regardless of her faith" (Sims 2021). Although she found success as an Olympic fencer, her hijab set her apart from some of her teammates.

Muhammed isn't the first or only Muslim woman to experience conflict between religious apparel and sporting uniforms. In her book, *Religion and Sports*, Rebecca Alpert details the story of Wojdan Ali Seraj Abdulrahim Shahrkhani who represented Saudi Arabia in the 2012 Olympic games in London (2015, pp. 134–142). While competing in judo, Shahrkani planned to compete wearing a hijab, but the International Judo Federation (IJF) deemed it a safety hazard and outside judo standards. A compromise was reached, and Shahrkani wore a tight-fitting cap and adjusted her uniform to cover her neck. Likewise, Muslim-American high school runner Noor Alexandria Abukaram was disqualified during a track meet in Ohio because she failed to obtain a religious waiver for wearing her hijab while running (Jones 2022). Abukaram used her experience as motivation to work toward changing the laws in her home state regarding religious symbols during high school athletic events.

Although these examples are drawn from the Islamic tradition, there are other examples where religious modesty standards come into conflict with sporting attire, like that of Pentecostal Christian and Jewish athletes refusing to wear shorts during athletic competitions. A long list of illustrations could be compiled showing the conflict between religious and sporting uniforms. Usually, some committee or leadership board must adjudicate whether a religious exemption can be extended in individual cases. These considerations must weigh individual religious freedoms against the regulations of sporting leagues and institutions.

> For further discussion, take the time to consider or discuss the following questions:
>
> - What other examples exist of religious athletes refusing to comply with sporting uniform regulations? Feel free to use the Internet to search for real-world case studies.
> - Where do you stand on these issues? Do you typically side with the sporting regulations or the religious athlete's rights? Why?
> - Are religious exemptions warranted in these cases? Why or why not?
> - Can you think of a specific sporting situation where a religious exemption should never be granted?

RELIGIOUS TRESPASS OR LIBERTY?

As these cases demonstrate, some athletes choose not to compartmentalize their personal religious commitments and display their religious expressions inside of sporting spaces. The focus of this chapter highlights examples supplied of Muslim athletes displaying their religiosity through prayer, attire, articulation, and religiously-inspired political stances. These are not exhaustive, and other cases could be detailed from other sports and religions. The sheer diversity of individual athletes across the globe produces an infinite pool of potential cases to study.

Conceptually, in this chapter, we aim to study these as religions in sports. Thinking about these two phenomena as distinctive categories opens a way to explore these expressions analytically. Some athletes perceive their religiosity as a key part of their identity and life that cannot be reduced to designated religious spaces. These athletes' religious expressions, not contained within religious domains, get carried into sporting spaces along with other aspects of the player's life. Some might argue that athletes shouldn't need or have to segment their racial or gender identity when within arenas, pitches, or fields, so why should they have to do so with religiosity?

Taken together this brings up a difficult question: should religious expressions ever be brought into sports? There exist different responses to this question. These responses often hinge on the extent of secular influence. Secular refers, at a minimum, to a diminishing reliance on religious authority. Governments can be secularly constructed – religious authority is minimized in comparison to the legal authority granted to government offices and positions. Marriage and divorce ceremonies, although performed at a religious site, are administered and recorded in government offices, for instance. The ultimate legal authority rests with local and state offices. Societies can operate secularly. This means members of a society tacitly or explicitly agree that religion should be private. This does not mean individuals have to eliminate their religiosity in favor of absolute atheism. However, within the public realm, it is expected that individuals would not use their religious ideas to make a political argument or use their religiosity to infringe upon others. There is much variety in how far this secular sentiment extends. In some secular societies, there are legal restrictions forbidding any government official to wear any religious symbol while conducting official state business. Publicly displaying a religious symbol, like a Christian crucifix or a Star of David, would be considered crossing over a secular line in these contexts. There is a spectrum of secular policies across the globe, and secular ideas, regulations, and social norms exist in great variety.

A key foundation of secular ideas is that religion can be private and internal. If the broad understanding is that religion exists primarily as a belief system getting practiced in religious spaces, then the argument follows that those elements can be partitioned off from public life. Public life includes politics and spaces where citizens gather to discuss shared issues. As there is no shared universal notion of religion, those proposing a secular stance understand religious positions as less helpful in reaching a social consensus on matters. Take, for instance, the issue of marriage. Many religions prescribe how and when marriages should occur. Some religions require members to only wed members of the religious group and disallow certain marriages (i.e., same sex marriages). For pluralistic societies, the government cannot regulate all marriages to conform to a specific religious tradition. Thus, a secular society requires citizens to record marriages with the state, but also permits individuals to have private marriage ceremonies of their liking. If a citizen, in a public debate, proposed a uniform marriage requirement for all citizens based on that citizen's religious devotion, most members of secular societies would find the proposal absurd or divisive. Why? Because without a shared reliance on a particular religious authority, contemporary societies typically govern without religious authority.

Secular societies, to be clear, are not anti-religion necessarily, although some religious people might make this argument. From the government's position, individual citizens have the religious liberty to explore a single or multiple religious institutions, rites, and rituals. Yet, the government must conduct politics in a way best suited for the majority of its members. Again, since no shared universal religious foundation exists, religious ideas and positions are inferior to data-driven scientific positions and rational argumentation. Some religious members of society, but not all religious members, might perceive this notion as anti-religious. For individuals who hold their religious ideas and foundations as universal for all humans, even the suggestion that scientific data and positions are superior to religious ones is offensive and carries an appearance of discrimination.

Knowing more about secular society enables us to engage better with our initial question regarding whether religious expressions should enter into sporting spaces. From a strict secular standpoint, the response probably leans toward not permitting religious expressions into sporting arenas. This is because sporting spaces are public spaces and are shared by the members of that society. Foundationally, religions should remain in private, religiously-designated spaces like mosques, churches, or temples from this viewpoint. Some people and sports fans holding a secular position might even find bringing religious expressions into sporting spaces divisive. Again, if there does not exist a commonly-held religious foundation, then some could understand an expression of particular religiosity as divisive to individuals not of that religious tradition. If one purpose of the sporting event is to unite fans around a particular team, religions could introduce an element to disrupt that unity. Some fans don't want their games or sports polluted or corrupted by religious expressions. These fans might not be opposed to religions or religious liberty but opposed to religion within sports. From the vantage point of the sports league or institution, religious expressions could introduce a controversy that the institution would need to address. This could be understood as a public relations headache. The secular position partitions sports, like government, as separate from religions as a safer strategy for all citizens and members of society. Another consideration in this debate would think about the overall health of the entire team. If a team member continually attempts to express their religious devotions in public or even to other teammates, this could lead to division or problems. From a fan, team, and management perspective, any disruption to the team internally could introduce disharmony and negatively influence the overall goal of team success. Religious expression is a negative encroachment into sporting spaces from this position.

Even within some secular societies, some fans might see no issue with athletes making small religious gestures while playing the sport. These gestures could include pointing to the heavens or making the Christian sign of the cross. Understood as individual religious liberty, there is probably a limit to how far individual athletes can publicly display their religiosity while playing. In this case, religious identity is an inseparable aspect of the player's life. This is still a secular position. Athletes can make a religious gesture or pray for themselves, which is still individualized based on the idea that religion is personal and private. From this stance, what wouldn't be permitted necessarily is an athlete leading the entire stadium of fans in a religious ritual or prayer. An act like this would extend into a public demonstration that infringes on the rights of others. From this vantage point, the fans and management are quite agnostic to the small gestures of religious devotion expressed within sporting spaces taking a "no harm, no foul" position.

In certain circumstances, even within secular societies, some members, typically religious themselves, perceive religious freedom as the ultimate of liberties. Thus, from this perspective any attempt to limit religious expression is discriminatory. Thus, these individual athletes, like all other members of society, should be able to express themselves religiously within sporting spaces, and all spaces for that matter. Religion, in this sense, is a holistic part of the individual's life and, thus, cannot be cordoned off. If the secular argument is to leave your religion at the door as one enters a public space, then this counterargument is that this is simply untenable. Religious individuals, from this perspective, simply cannot comply with the secular practice and should not be forced to do so. Hence, some fans of Tim Tebow not only supported Tebowing but wanted Tebow to express his religiosity even more. Likewise, many religious fans supported Olajuwon's devotion to fasting. Religious liberty and freedom supersede secular intentions to protect public spaces. The question often leveled to those maintaining this position is whether they would be willing to allow all religious expressions, including those with which they disagree, to enter publicly in sporting spaces.

Whether religious expressions should be permitted into sporting spaces depends on numerous considerations. The political positions of individuals within secular societies and the norms practiced within those societies will determine much of what occurs in relation to this matter. Some secular societies limit religious expressions to designated religious spaces. The rules would be quite different in other countries with different types of governments, like with a theocratic or communist regime of power. A theocratic government would likely permit those religious expressions in sporting spaces that align with their religious positions but potentially ban all other expressions. A communist government would likely censor any and all religious expressions in public places, including sporting arenas. Much will depend on the political context in which the sporting event occurs.

CHAPTER SYNTHESIS

This chapter highlights how some athletes' religiosity affects their actions within sporting spaces. The examples described show how some religious expressions are received well and often approved by society and the media, and other religious gestures critiqued as unacceptable. In the age of the Internet and mass communication technologies, athletes must weigh how much of their religious devotion to publicly display during sporting events or on their social media accounts. Being open with religiosity could lead to an increase or a reduction in fan support depending on the circumstances. Also, sporting institutions sometimes regulate the limits of religious expressions. Like the examples involving the hijab, organizations can step in to make decisions for athletes. Not all religious expressions or attire are appropriate or safe for specific spaces. From a foundational perspective, this illustrates how religions sometimes encroach into sports. Not all fans or citizens agree with religiosity within sports events. Secular views often insist that religion remains private or not public while potentially permitting a certain level of individual religious expression. Thoughts on this topic will depend on societal norms and personal understandings of religious freedom.

More broadly, adopting the religions in sports perspective requires compartmentalizing concepts, categories, and domains. Religions are independent of sports and *vice versa*, but religiosity is brought into sporting spaces by some athletes. In the next chapter, we investigate the opposite: sports in religion. In this approach, we still adopt the distinctive categories approach. As we progress through this book, we will challenge this, but this is the typical way people in Western countries think about these phenomena.

RECOMMENDED READING

The framework of religions within sports provides a wonderful time to consider religiosity from the athlete's perspective. Some athletes publish autobiographical works that share how their religious devotion intersects with their athletic pursuits. Referenced with this chapter, Hakeem Olajuwon's (1996) *Living the Dream: My Life and Basketball* and Ibtihaj Muhammed's (2018) *Proud: My Fight for an Unlikely American Dream* detail from a Muslim-American perspective what it's like to be a professional athlete, follower of Islam, and American. Tim Tebow has published numerous self-help books and an autobiographical account titled *Through My Eyes* (2011). Reading and comparing these biographical accounts would open numerous conversations. Additional accounts from athletes share their backgrounds and experiences within sports and how religion and faith played a role in their achievements.

In addition, numerous religious studies scholars take on the task of theorizing how and when religions enter into sporting spheres. Along with Rebecca Alpert's (2015) *Religion and Sports: An Introduction and Case Studies*, I recommend Alpert's co-edited volume with Arthur Remillard (2019), *Gods, Games, and Globalization: New Perspectives on Religion and Sport*. Both of these books provide excellent case studies and questions around religions in sports, amongst other issues. *Religion and Sports in North America: Critical Essays for the Twenty-First Century* (2022), edited by Jeffrey Scholes and Randall Balmer, offers interesting case studies of religions in sports while considering how globalization and commercialization, amongst other contributing factors, influence sports.

SPORTS IN RELIGIONS

In the previous chapter, we examined instances in which athletes express their religiosity within sporting spaces. These include visible expressions like prayer and less visible instances like fasting. Some of the religious expressions cause very little disruption to team play while others could be problematic. As these displays become publicized, athletes, fans, and organizations must decide how to adjudicate individual situations. In addition to sports organizations' protocols, the media and fans serve as a public filter that determines the public acceptability of specific religious moves in sporting spaces. Within the limited number of examples included in the last chapter, questions emerge around uniformity, secular stances, and the possible conflict created with individual expressions of religion in sporting spaces.

As a reminder, the approach to the last chapter was religions *in* sports. In that approach, religions and sports are two distinct cultural phenomena that are fairly easy to demarcate. Within this chapter, we will invert the previous approach and examine how some religious groups utilize, adopt, create, and organize sports to further their objectives. In other words, we'll explore sports *in* religions. We first examine the popularity of sports across the globe. Noting the benefits of sports for individuals and collectives establishes a foundation for better understanding why some religious groups choose to adopt sports, paying particular attention to Christian and Jewish examples. After reviewing some social benefits of sports participation and two examples of religious communities adapting sports for distinctive purposes, we briefly consider the role of power in each scenario. In sum, power dynamics, like

DOI: 10.4324/9781003362630-3

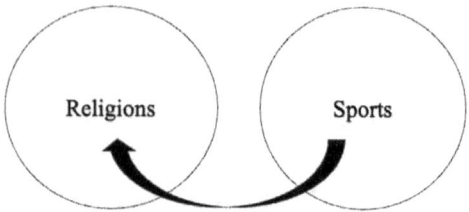

Figure 3.1

most cultural phenomena, significantly influence certain strategies and motivations in religions and sports.

To once again visualize this approach, Figure 3.1's oversimplified illustration denotes the idea that religions and sports exist as distinctive things in the world with sports operating sometimes within religious spaces. The *sports in religions* approach continues to assume the distinctiveness of sports and religions. In the following chapter, we'll interrogate this assumption, but, for now, we will continue the assumption that these two cultural phenomena are related but unmistakable.

THE GLOBAL POPULARITY OF SPORTS

Across the globe, sports play a significant role in the lives of billions of people. In fact, it is difficult in many places to not come in contact with sports in some fashion. The IPSOS's 2021 report indicates a large swathe of the global population participates in some form of exercise or sporting activities each week (Global Views on Sports and Exercise 2021). In 2021, estimates approximated that about ⅔ of those within the United States participated in a sport with a massive increase in women playing sports (Broughton 2022). The European Commission estimates that over half of Europeans exercise or participate in sports regularly (Broughton 2022). Numerous components of sports exist: individual participation, child development, fandom, business profits, employment, and media coverage. These aspects of sports draw people into playing and different disciplinary scholars study these elements. Reviewing some of these aspects and the associated research helps show the value of sports and, eventually, why religious communities might consider adopting and adapting sports to fulfill their needs.

One key aspect of sports is individual competition and participation. Everyday people organize games in local gyms, fields, and pitches hoping to compete in the games they enjoy. Whether a pickup game or an organized league match, people tend to ascribe significant value to these games with recognized benefits to playing sports: competition, skill improvement, and cardiovascular exercise. Being able to compete with others pushes individuals to improve their abilities, dexterity, and skills. Scholars within the fields of kinesiology, psychology, and leisure management study these human activities and their consequences. Friendly competition fuels friendships and cultivates relationships (Legg et al. 2017), although some competition results in negative health consequences (Giza et al. 2017). Playing sports comes with health benefits as well including physiological, psychological, and social health (Andersen et al. 2019). In a world where a vast number of people work sedentary jobs, sitting at desks, staring at computer screens, the physical movement of sports counterbalances a long day at the office. Playing sports allows individuals to disconnect from the stresses of life to focus attention on competition. For individuals around the globe, sports offer a healthy escape from other aspects of life.

The importance of sports is exemplified through the number of parents who encourage their children to play sports. Many reasons could compel parents to want their kids to play sports, and researchers investigate, and often prescribe, sports participation for youth, like encouraging active lifestyles at an early age. With the popularity of smartphones and video gaming devices, some parents worry their children commit unhealthy amounts of time to staring inactively at screens. Some children might display an early aptitude for specific sports, and parents see a potential future as an athlete for their children. Professional sports contracts are lucrative and parents might dream of a comfortable life for their children's future. Although there are some horror stories of parents pushing kids too hard to play sports, many parents enjoy watching their kids score a soccer goal, make a basketball shot, or a volleyball serve. Studies support parent intuition to enroll children in team sports as they show that sports participation leads to better physical health for children and youth (Telford et al. 2016). Other studies show increased child and parent communication during sports participation (Dorsch et al. 2015). These parents might enroll their children in sports to learn life lessons like how to navigate wins and losses. Children also learn strategies related to team communication, unity, and working together with others (Holt et al. 2017). In sum, a wonderful element of parenting often involves watching, coaching, and supporting children's participation in sports, which also comes with numerous cognitive, physical, and emotional benefits for the child.

Beyond physically participating as a sporting player, numerous people across the globe involve themselves with sports through spectating, fandom, and product consumption. Spectating at live sporting events, online streams, or via television allows billions of people to tune into live sporting championship events like the FIFA World Cup, NFL Super Bowl, or NHL Stanley Cup. Gathering together to watch these events cultivates community around shared sports affinities and teams (Kalman-Lamb 2021). A spectrum of fandom levels exists with some avid fans wearing sports uniforms, committing to watching all games with other fans, or examining team statistics. Sports create an opportunity for shared experiences in countries where politics and religion, for example, polarize. In one research project I conducted with people leaving their families' faith tradition, it surprised me to hear how many identified sports fandom as a remaining shared and safer place for interactions with families (Shoemaker 2019). Moreover, many sports fans gather together across racial, ethnic, and gender divides.

In addition to the individual, parent, and fan benefits, the sports industry and business constitutes one of the largest global markets. Sports operate commercially and transnationally with team and player products sold across the globe. Individual athletes now commonly sign million-dollar contracts. Teams and countries build massive arenas and stadiums to accommodate consumers desperately wanting to witness their favorite team and players perform. Countries capitalize on tourists incorporating sporting events into their holiday and vacation plans (Kim et al. 2015). The rise of esports, sports gambling, and fantasy sports only serves to increase attention to the sporting world (Ruihley et al. 2021). The global sports industry reshapes numerous other economic aspects

(Sage 2010). Furthermore, the sports industry creates numerous job opportunities. Universities offer academic pathways to specialize in sports management, sports journalism, sports marketing, and sports training and coaching. Sports equal financial opportunities for people around the world.

With the ubiquity of sports across the globe, people, whether sports fans or not, find themselves inundated with sports images, broadcasts, events, and celebrities. Twenty-four hour news media sources provide commentary, replays, and analysis of sporting events daily. Billboards, advertisements, and commercials congest the airwaves, social media, and cities. Celebrity athletes appear in commercials advocating for particular products (some sports-related; others not). Magazines, newspapers, and online news sources cover athletes' personal lives and activities. These sources print positive team accomplishments along with negative scandals or missteps, with average fans adding their opinions on the matters. Summarily, it would be difficult to avoid sports in many societies today.

The studies referenced in the previous paragraphs represent only the smallest fraction of sports studies. With the popularity and global dimensions of sports continuing to thrive, social scientists, psychologists, economists, kinesiologists, and humanities scholars offer numerous studies regarding the facets of sports in societies. These studies, like those offered in the field of religious studies, contribute to understanding the human experience as it relates to games, play, and competition. Also grasping the import of sports, some religious communities see sports as a potential resource to meet their organization's objectives. In the following, we inspect some case studies involving religious communities using sports for specific purposes. In each of these cases, sport is a tool – a mechanism to accomplish goals. In the subsequent cases, sports remain secondary to religious devotion.

BOX 3.1 SCHOLARSHIP SEARCH

Scholars of various fields across the globe design research projects to analyze sports, games, and play. These studies contain a vast range of topics related to sports studies. Various methods, approaches, and geographical context generate a corpus of learned material contributing to an overall perspective on sports and human experiences. In addition to the methodological distinctiveness of these projects, most research projects concentrate on a very definitive context, demographics, and procedures. These nuances might consist of various age ranges (youth, adult, mature adults), gender differences or similarities, racial contrasts or resemblances, amateur and/or professional levels of competition, urban or rural, transnational comparisons, international analyses, past experiences, current activities, future plans, and other correlative conditions. A researcher must try to account for all contributing factors potentially affecting the outcome of their research design.

Once a researcher or a team of researchers completes a project, they typically share the results of their data collection. This takes many forms in the contemporary world, like podcasting results or sharing on a public platform like TheConversation.com. However, the primary way to share results is to publish their work in an academic journal. An academic journal is different from a newspaper article or blog posting because of the peer review processes that research summaries undergo. Peer review involves other scholars within the field examining, critiquing, and commenting on the final, written accounts of a research project. The written accounts typically summarize the details of the project – research inquiry, method, data, analysis, argumentation, and conclusions. Given all the details, a peer reviewer adjudicates the techniques, analysis, and results of the research, verifying their legitimacy and accuracy. Peer reviewing involves rigorous scrutiny as scholars intend to maintain the credibility of their field of study. This critical posture is aided by the fact that most reviewing is conducted anonymously, providing the reviewer the ability to be honest and critical. Although not absolutely perfect, the academic process of sharing data and results furnishes students and scholars with verifiable data related to specific topics.

A worthwhile exercise involves examining two or more academic studies related to similar sports topics. Some university or college students reading this should have access to numerous academic journals in their libraries. For others, Google Scholar provides access to most article titles and full access to numerous articles. Take some time to conduct a search on a topic of your interests related to sports. I recommend making this as specific as possible. For instance, instead of searching for "sports South America," try refining the approach with something like "volleyball Brazil youth." Searching for "volleyball Brazil youth" yielded, for example, the following two accessible articles:

"Differences in Game Patterns Between Male and Female Youth Volleyball" summarizes a gendered examination of youth volleyball games conducted by Gustavo Costa, José Afonso, Erika Brant, and Isabel Mesquita (2012). This research team determined some baseline differences between how young men and women play volleyball.

"Performance Analysis of U19 Male and Female Setters in the Brazilian Volleyball Championship Teams" explores one specific volleyball position – the setter – in one division of volleyball (under 19) in Minas Gerais and São Paulo. This study, conducted by Cristino J. A. Matias, Jara González-Silva, M. Perla Moreno, and Pablo J. Greco analyzed setting variables for male and female teams including the setting conditions, tempo, and number of attackers available to set (2021).

Although both studies focus on male and female volleyball comparison in Brazil, each project employs different methods and categories to conduct the respective studies, selecting different age groups and regions of Brazil, and adopting different focal points of volleyball techniques and skills. Both articles detail the methods, data collection, and analysis of the project along with identifying limitations of the research. A similar project could adopt the techniques of these researchers and examine youth volleyball in Europe or Asia, for instance. In a different direction, these research methods could be applied to other youth sports.

To complete this exercise, use a library resource or Google Scholar to search for two or more sports studies research articles published in academic journals. What kinds of research are found and what specifics are analyzed? What are the commonalities of the research or where do they diverge?

SPORTS AS A PROSELYTIZING TOOL

In 1963, Billy Graham delivered nightly sermons to thousands of people in southern California. Graham, who was a rural North Carolina preacher, found popularity traveling across the United

States, and eventually internationally, to deliver an evangelical Protestant message of afterlife salvation, which he called "new birth" resulting in a "peace with God" (Wacker 2014, p. 34). His prominence extended beyond religious domains into the political spheres as he held private meetings with American presidents leading to the title, "America's Pastor." In the southern California crusades, as they were called, Graham stuck to his typical sermon script imploring attendees to adopt his message of saying a sinner's prayer and converting to the Protestant branch of Christianity. Graham meticulously outlined a path to an eternal life in a heavenly realm after one's physical death on this planet. However Graham's message promised results in this life as well. If people sincerely accepted his message and followed the salvation plan as presented, they would find meaning in living lives devoid of alcohol, drug, and sex dependence. Southern Californians heavily embraced Graham's message with thousands converting and many more thousands attending his daily events.

Interestingly, Graham found success delivering his crusades, not in the typical church building, but within sports stadiums. With the sheer number of attendees, Graham's team had to consider an appropriate venue to hold his meetings. In 1957, Graham's team filled Yankee Stadium in New York City for daily services. Richard Nixon, then Vice President, extended greetings from the Oval Office at one meeting. For three weeks in 1963, Graham delivered these sermons in Anaheim Stadium, home of the Los Angeles Angels. He would return to this venue again to deliver sermons through the 1980s. A key aspects of these events included professional athletes professing their faith in Christianity and Graham's mission. Also in the 1980s, Graham utilized Sheffield's Bramall Lane stadium as part of his Mission England crusade. Graham's events exemplified the religions in sporting spaces approach. With Graham's success, some within the Protestant tradition imagined how sports might be a potential resource for expanding their membership base.

Within some religious traditions, like Graham's evangelical Protestantism, recruiting and converting new members into the religious community remains a major objective. Those within the religious tradition trust the foundational premises of their tradition and are compelled to attempt to convince others to change their perspectives. The attempt to persuade a person to convert to a different religious ideology is known as proselytizing. Various forms of proselytizing exist. This could include formal methods (sermons, printed materials, advertisements) or informal approaches (one on one conversations). Some religious communities train their members on how to conduct proselytizing strategies. Some Christian subgroups like Jehovah's Witness and the Church of Jesus Christ of Latter-day Saints are known for their intentional training and deployment of members for proselytizing agendas. Proselytizing varies across particular nation states and regions due to cultural and legal norms within those areas.

Other preachers, witnessing Graham's success, mimicked his simplified sermon message, his delivery style, and his usage of public, sporting venues. Decades later, for instance, Promise Keepers, a men's Christian group, held massive gatherings in sporting venues across the United States. With the popularity of sports and the successful usage of sporting venues by Billy Graham's team, some Christian innovators go further and fashion sports as a proselytizing tool. In the mid-20th century, after some Christians feared that sports actually lured people away from faith or church commitments, "the [American] church started to re-engage the world of sport, recognizing the potential of impacting the world for Christ through sports outreach" (Tucker and Woodbridge 2012, p. 1). These efforts became known as "sports ministry," signifying the usage of sports to conduct the work of evangelizing, or converting, people to the Christian faith. Beyond evangelism, several other Christian theological foundations support sports as a means for Christian participation. Theologians and sports ministers Tim Tucker and Noel Woodbridge identify sports as related to creation, worship, redemption, and liberty within their explanation of sports ministry, and discovered that a significant portion of their survey sample identified evangelism as the ultimate usage of sports by Christian communities (Tucker and Woodbridge 2012). Within the United States, sports ministries are exceptionally popular. Annie Blazer notes,

> There are now over 100 sports ministry organizations in the United States that involve tens of thousands of athletes, coaches, and fans. There is a sport ministry organization for nearly every imaginable sport, from basketball and soccer to surfing and rodeo. The two largest sports ministry organizations remain the multi-sport ministries of Fellowship of Christian Athletes (FCA) and Athletes in Action (AIA), which have yearly revenue incomes of $141 million and $37 million respectively.
>
> (2019)

With both the recognized utility of sports and the potential revenue generation of sports ministry, athletes, churches, and parachurch organizations have much to gain in employing sports as an evangelical tool.

Whereas Graham simply used sporting venues to host his large services, some para-Christian groups maintain a specific agenda of embedding religiosity within sports. Upward Sports (www.upward.org) is one such organization focusing on youth sports. As stated earlier, many parents seek sports leagues for their children. Upward Sports offers youth leagues with a promise of a stress-free atmosphere for children to develop their skills. They offer basketball, football, and cheerleading leagues. With the highly competitive sports industry in the United States, it is easy to imagine parents would welcome a less stressful space for their children to learn how to play particular sports. Yet, Upward Sports not only strives to supply less stressful fields and courts, they intend "to use the power of sports to share the gospel and promote the discovery of Jesus in every community." They accomplish this by embedding religious training and proselytizing in children's games. During weekly practices, participating kids learn to memorize bible verses and hear Christian messages. In some of the kids' games, a church member shares their religious story with audience members at the halftime point of the game. As team players and coaches gather to rehydrate and re-strategize, and spectators restock on drinks and snacks at the intermission of the game, a Christian member attempts to convert audience members. The intention then is to transform sporting events into religious opportunities.

Similar to Upward Sports in mission, the Christian Wrestling Federation (CWF) exists "to be a Christian outreach ministry that shares the love of Jesus Christ, through wrestling events around the world" (https://christianwrestling.com/about-2/). The CWF uses the popularity of professional wrestling entertainment to extend the proselytizing call for Christians. Wrestlers, like Jesus Freak and the Bishop, compete in staged wrestling events mirroring larger organizations like World Wrestling Entertainment (WWE), but with a twist. CWF wrestlers compete for championship belts, employ cheating and other methods to win, and display their athletic abilities through feats of strength and agility. At some point during the wrestling event, however, a member of the CWF offers their religious story to the audience in hopes of convincing them to convert to Christianity. Often these wrestlers build upon their personas to deliver the message. For example, if the wrestling character cheats in order to win, the CWF wrestler might discuss the immortality of the character they play, and how converting to Christianity compels people to be morally better. In addition, the wrestlers eagerly admit that the wrestling portion of the event, including their character personas, are entertainment and fictional; however, the important part of the event remains the evangelistic message promoted by the wrestlers and the CWF organization.

The two examples of CWF and Upward Sports illustrate how sports can be utilized as a strategic mechanism to further the membership recruitment and religious expansion efforts of some Christian denominations, communities, and parachurch organizations. By providing safe spaces for youth to play sports like basketball and flag football, Upward Sports embeds a Christian proselytizing priority in league practices and games. The CWF co-opts the spectacle aspects of sports as a draw for fans who want to watch professional wrestlers entertain. Integrated into the entertainment is a serious time for Christians to advance their theologies regarding salvation and an afterlife. In these instances, people get to play and watch sports, but there's a religious intent within the sports. Although different in technique, these two sports ministries both maintain the same goal of proselytizing those outside of the Protestant Christian tradition. Moreover, sports ministries are an extension of historical efforts, like Billy Graham's outreach efforts, to compel others to convert to their faith system.

BOX 3.2 CONVERTING SPORTS?

The largest group of conservative Christians within the United States fall into the evangelical category. Using data from the 2020 Census, the Public Religion Research Institute (PRRI) estimates that around 14% of American society identifies as evangelical. This represents a decline in those identifying as evangelical compared to about 23% in 2006. Even with the decline, over 1 in 10 Americans identify with evangelicalism. David Bebbington (1989) argues that evangelicals concentrate on four items: biblicism (all religious truths found in this text); crucicentrism (Jesus atoned for humankind with his crucifixion); conversionism (understanding that all humans need to be converted); and activism (evangelicals should actively share their message of Jesus with others). Based on the first two, biblicism and crucicentrism, evangelicals (those who have experienced a conversion), should fervently attempt to convert others, which will ultimately lead to a social transformation (as envisioned by evangelicals). American evangelicals, since the late 1970s, have embraced an emphasis on mobilizing politically to mold the United States into adopting evangelical morals and principles within its policy decisions. Whether one agrees with evangelical attempts or not, it is difficult to ignore the impact evangelicals have had on American society.

When certain domains do not reflect evangelical principles, evangelicals simply create versions that reflect their values. As a key aspect of the activist and conversion agenda, evangelicalism, at least within the United States, offers several alternatives for non-Christian events and activities. For example, the Christian music industry within the United States is a thriving industry offering Christian versions of rock, rap, and country music. The Christian alternative mimics popular artists and sounds, while lyrically the music might discuss salvation, Protestant living standards, or social issues from a conservative Christian perspective. In other words, these Christians understand popular music as needing a lyrical makeover. Bands like Casting Crowns and Hillsong United offer a rock 'n' roll sound with a softer message of Jesus' love.

In a sense, conservative Christians *convert* popular forms of music to further their cause. Like converting individuals into Protestant Christianity, some conservative Christians embrace the notion of converting popular culture into Christian subculture. For those unfamiliar, there exists numerous examples of Christian alternatives to nonreligious phenomena. These include the American Heritage Girls (www.americanheritagegirls.org), which is a substitute for the Girl Scouts of America (www.girlscouts.org). American Heritage Girls, like the Girl Scouts of America, offers camping and outdoor activities for young girls, badges to be earned, and uniforms, along with an emphasis on conservative Christian principles. Another example is the conservative Christian GodTube (www.godtube.com), a "platform offering online Christian videos with faith-based, family friendly content." This supplies conservative Christians with a different option to the more popular YouTube (www.youtube.com) site, which hosts millions of videos of various kinds. The Christian alternative industry extends into numerous domains of life like Christian options for medical care and social media.

In the previous section, we examined the ways in which sports get employed as a tool for proselytizing efforts. With a few simple modifications, wrestling and youth sports leagues transform in evangelizing spaces. To take the assessment further, we need to grapple with the notion that the sports are being converted instead of simply being a resource for evangelism. Like a building being consecrated for religious usage, sports are potentially consecrated for divine purposes. Alternatively, consider the consecration process of bread and wine within some Christian communities. The loaf of bread and wine, two ordinary objects, transform into something sacred once a priest or minister blesses or sanctifies them. The consecration processes vary, but, typically, simply include an ordained, or recognized, religious authority to pray or articulate a blessing. At this point, the ordinary becomes extraordinary, or the ordinary transforms into the sacred – the nonreligious becomes religious.

If we take this to be true, then we must consider if sports are converted in these processes. If there is a conversion of sports into a religious tool for proselytizing, do the sports transform into something beyond the ordinary? If places (i.e., buildings) and objects (i.e., bread and wine) can be consecrated, can sports also be consecrated? Once consecrated, does the essence of the sport change? Or stated differently, with sports repurposed with religious objectives, are the sports transformed into an extraordinary phenomenon? Who gets to decide?

SPORTS AS AN INTEGRATION TOOL

Although social media greatly expands an individual's social networks, people tend to operate with a much smaller social network in their daily life. Kinship and friendship often define our closest relationships. People often maintain the strongest commitments to their closest companions or family members, creating a tribal formation. Social scientists and social psychologists refer to these tight networks as one's ingroup. The ingroup represents the people with whom an individual would identify as part of their tribe. To belong in a tribe provides a baseline approach to understanding the world through shared categories. These "social categories should be treated both as a perception of social structure and a cognitive mechanism participating in its reproduction" (Shkurko 2014, p. 189). In other words, the ingroup/outgroup thought processes are ways of perceiving reality and tend to reproduce reality for the individual. Shared histories, experiences, and cultural norms bind the ingroup together. This tribe isn't perfect and intergroup conflict will more than likely emerge at some point; however, the ingroup defines itself over and against an outgroup. In short, the ingroup knows who they are by comparing themselves to a different group. Ingroup and outgroup thinking works at multiple levels – family, local, national, and global. A member of one country might, at certain moments, defend members of their country and staunchly criticize the cultures and norms of other countries based on the cognitive categories they hold. This develops ingroup biases against people from the outgroup, which can lead to several negative social consequences. This ingroup position might lead to wars or other conflicts. For good or bad, ingroups and outgroups tend to be the common approach to relationship networks.

It is easy to apply ingroup and outgroup theory to religions and sports. Both sports and religions fundamentally create a group with which one identifies and often positions an outgroup as antagonistic. Sports fans proudly know exactly which ingroup team they belong to but also know emphatically which tribal team they consider a threat to their success. One's success is dependent, quite frankly, on a different group's failure to succeed. The ingroup dynamics of sports teams creates an easy way to identify tribal members as well. If someone wears your team's jersey, an immediate recognition emerges of similarities: these two people share something and reside in the same ingroup. On the other hand, if an individual sees someone wearing a rival team's jersey, negative emotions (hatred, distrust, etc.) emerge. In fact, one study shows how in some instances, the opposing team's failure trumps the ingroup team's success (Lehr et al. 2019). Likewise, religions architect ingroup/outgroup dynamics with cultural, ritual, and theological boundaries. As religions form intense identities between people based on beliefs, values, and adopted cultural norms, with a definitive confidence around these practices and beliefs based on a supernatural understanding, those outside can be considered impure, negatively different, or even as heretics. To be clear, religions and sports aren't unique in the creation of ingroup/outgroup categories; humans tend to live with a tribal mentality of us versus them. Yet, sports and religions are two instruments used to qualify who members of the tribe are and are not.

Not all ingroup/outgroup boundaries operate rigidly or definitively however. Moments exist when people traverse the ingroup/outgroup establishments, expanding the limits of who is accepted or rejected in the ingroup/outgroup. Just as sports and religions often serve to establish ingroup or outgroup markers, these two phenomena can also supply an opportunity for people to break though divisions for more integration into society. Sports potentially serve as a tool for integration, which consists of both negative and positive connotations. Negatively, some colonizing nations utilized sports as a means of subversively acculturating indigenous peoples. This returns us to the idea of proselytizing discussed previously. Under the guise of proselytization, Christian colonizers attempted to "co-opt indigenous peoples into British imperial civilization, to produce 'acceptable natives,' and thus sport was employed in this context as a social integrator of sorts" (Magdalinski and Chandler 2002, p. 5). In this context, colonizers adapted sports to manipulate indigenous peoples into converting to Christianity and adopting British cultural norms. From a top-down perspective, these nation states co-opted sports. However, sports also offer a form of agency for individuals and groups attempting to acculturate themselves into new societies.

Introducing a new people-group into an established society often unfortunately results in negative experiences for new members. Different physical appearances, cultural norms, and languages set apart the new group as foreign or strange. Not everyone within the established community is eager to willingly and easily accept the new group. The ingroup resists outgroup integration. For example, consider the experiences of some Jewish peoples across the globe who experience discrimination and ostracization. Although numerous distinctions exist, many people categorize all Jewish people as a racial group who are biologically different, leading to antisemitism and stereotyping (Dart 2021). Conspiracy theories abound regarding Jewish people, their sacred text, and history, with some promoting the idea that Jewish people are members of a secret society bent on establishing a new, world government (Douglas et al. 2019). These unfounded conspiracy theories and stereotypes plague Jewish integration efforts in the contemporary world and have created problems throughout history.

One prevailing stereotype purports that "Jews don't play sports." This stereotype casts Jewish people as odd or unathletic. However, one sociological study discovered that Jewish participants of the study "were quick to disabuse the suggestion that sports were alien to Jewish culture" (p. 690). In fact, examples illustrate how Jewish people utilized sports as an integration mechanism into broader society upon immigrating. In the following, we examine two examples of Jewish integration through sport. These instances highlight how Jewish people utilized sports to learn more about the new society to which they immigrated and how sports provided a level of inclusivity not provided initially by the host society. These examples also demonstrate how sports provide an outlet for Jewish people to challenge baseless misunderstandings and find a cultural mechanism for integration.

As Jewish women immigrated into the United States, they found numerous misconceptions about their religiosity and ethnicity. At the same time, the new immigrants knew little about American life and norms. Organizations emerged and attempted to rectify both of these issues. The Young Women's Hebrew Association (YWHA), founded in New York City in 1902, served to enhance and uphold the spiritual and religious identity of women and girls as members of a Jewish team, organization, or club, yet at the same time offered occasions for them to participate in the growing sporting culture in American society.

(Borish 2002, p. 73)

Historian Linda Borish describes how various Jewish organizations in the United States provided a place for Jewish women to successfully become professional athletes, like golfer Elaine Rosenthal Einhardt and Olympic swimming champions Aileen Riigin and Helen Meaney. Einhardt, a member of the Illinois Golf Hall of Fame, won several championships across the country and "played in patriotic golf exhibitions and raised over $200,000 for the American Red Cross" (p. 84). As many organizations prohibited Jews and women from membership or participation, Jewish womens' organizations supplied a safe space for Jewish women to compete, practice, and improve their skills. Through competing in local, national, and international contests, these female Jewish athletes challenged both the incorrect stereotypes cast upon all Jewish people as unathletic and the often male-dominated sports spheres. These women "defied the early twentieth-century stereotype of the American Jew, especially of girls and women, who were thought to be lacking in physical health and disinterested in participating in sport" (Borish 2019, p. 166). Through sports competitions, Jewish women found cultural capital within a society suspicious of Jewish people. Moreover, these organizations provided a space for female Jewish athletes to "gain access to American cultural knowledge and activities" (p. 73) while "preserving their Jewish identity, contoured by their gender and ethnic roles in American society" (p. 90). In other words, sports participation centralized by the Jewish organization permitted a level of ingroup integration while also being able to maintain their particular religious, ethnic, and gender identities.

Like Jewish women, Jewish men encountered numerous biases against them. Thought to be "People of the book, not a People of the body," the stereotype of Jewish men as "unathletic and effeminate...persisted through Jewish history and [has] diminished but not disappeared even today" (Alpert 2014, p. 101). As Jewish women attempted to find a place for females in sports, Jewish men sought to prove their masculinity through their athleticism. In the 1920s, some Jewish men looked to the sport of boxing to prove their strength and manliness. Although Jewish men found some success earlier in boxing, for instance, Daniel Mendoza, the 18th boxing champion of England from 1792 to 1795, the 1920s and 1930s was a time of dominance by Jewish men in the boxing world. Benny Leonard held the lightweight championship for eight years (1917 to 1925) and three-time champion Barney Ross competed in multiple weight categories. Heavyweight champions like Max Baer rose to prominence in the 1930s in the United States and became "the ideal of virile manliness and bodily perfection" (Norwood 2009, p. 167). The success of these boxers chronologically aligns with a rise of antisemitism in Europe and the United States as eventually evidenced with the dominance of the Nazi Party and its vicious policies against Jews. Historian Stephen A. Norwood succinctly points out: "Boxing...allowed American Jews to dramatize their determination to fight back aggressively as antisemitism intensified both at home and abroad" (p. 187). At a time when Jewish male immigrants sought to prove their masculinity, they found the sport of boxing as the avenue for cultural acceptance.

Various sports served as an avenue for some Jewish people, both men and women, to assimilate into American society. Through playing sports, Jewish women defied the doubly troublesome idea that sports are no place for Jews or women. These women broke into spheres reserved for men and Gentiles. They paved an easier route for female athletes like WNBA (Women's Basketball Association) legend Sue Bird and Olympic skater Sasha Cohen. Jewish boxers used their boxing abilities to demonstrate their tenacity and vigor over and against the biases against Jewish men. Jewish male athletes compete in all major sports today and few question their abilities due to their religiosity. When an ingroup questions the acceptableness of a new outgroup, sports supply a path for those within the outgroup to demonstrate their abilities and find a level of cultural acceptance. These examples shouldn't gloss over or sanitize the difficulties and hardships faced by Jewish athletes throughout history though. Cultural integration processes remain challenging. Ingroup biases exist and result in social strains, but sports participation illustrates an outgroups' similarities with the ingroup.

BOX 3.3 GEOGRAPHY, SPORTS, RELIGION

In thinking about cultural assimilation and ingroup/outgroup dynamics, it is important to keep in mind how often sports and religions connect to specific places. With advances in globalization and communications, different sports and religions thrive across the globe, but, historically, each group favored their religions, sports, and teams. In fact, many people identify their ingroup with certain religious traditions and sports teams. This positions sports and religions as key cultural identifiers. People hold these phenomena as vital to their country and personal past, present, and future. In short, devoted people simply could not imagine life without their sports or religions. This makes religions and sports mechanisms for both resisting new group integrations and assimilating new people-groups into the broader community. As with the Jewish examples given in the previous section, sometimes sports serve as a way to prove an individual's contribution and similarity with the community.

Take a moment to do a search online for "map of the most popular sports around the globe." Several different attempts to map sports to locations should appear. These maps reflect people-groups and history. Soccer (or futbol) should appear as the most popular in a majority of countries worldwide. Other sports appear on the maps as well like American football, archery, rugby, and baseball. Now dive deeper into the investigation. Select a country and research which sports are the most popular in that country. Historically, when did the game appear? Was it invented in that country or imported? What was the integration of that sport like? How has the game been modified over the years? How is the game reflected in the weather patterns? For example, more northerly countries might tend to play more hockey due to longer, colder winters.

Now open multiple tabs in the search browser and search for "map of world religions." You'll find a similar color-coded map showing the largest religious identification in each country around the globe. Christianity and Islam are the largest religious affiliations, but a variety of religious traditions exist where Christianity and Islam dominate. As before, select a country and do further research. Was the dominant religious tradition imported or started within the selected country? Did colonialism play a role in importing or imposing the

> religious tradition? Did indigenous people initially resist or accept the religiosity? Is the religious tradition supported by the government or do citizens maintain more freedom of selection?
>
> Myriad questions could be researched about religions, sports, and specific places. Take some time to compare the sports map with the religions map. What if there was an overlay of the two maps? Where would they reflect correlations? For example, where is cricket the most popular and what are the dominant religious affiliations? Are these connected? What, if anything, is soccer's relationship with Christianity and Islam on the world map? What about more broadly on the Asian continent? What sports and religions appear? Are there connections or not? To take this even further, a research project involving a specific sport, religion, and geographical location could yield interesting results as it pertains to historical events, cultural development, gender roles, or economic development.

SPORTS, RELIGION, POWER DYNAMICS

When comparing the two examples supplied in this chapter, some readers might note the vast differences between the positionality of the religious communities and the expressed purposes for using sports. On one hand, the first example explores how Christians, the majority religious affiliation within the United States, utilize sports as a means of increasing their majority numerically. Again, to be clear, not all Christians approve of using sports in this method. However, some conservative Christians within the United States provide sports leagues for youth and adults with some of these leagues developed for proselytization. On the other hand, Jewish people, who still make up a very small percentage of the American population and continue to experience antisemitic attitudes, gestures, and actions, might participate in sports as a means to ameliorate negativity toward their religion and ethnicity and improve their social status. They maintain a minority position numerically and, often, a minoritized position socially and politically. In sum, the two examples demonstrate how power dynamics influence and inform the usage of sports.

Taking these two examples into consideration, we could begin to answer the ambitious question of whether religious communities should adopt sports in these manners. For the first example regarding Christian proselytization, some might consider this an abuse of sports or, more minimally, a manipulation of sports. Is it ethically appropriate for a religious community to employ sports as a converting mechanism? If an individual is invited to watch a friend or family member's child play in a league game, is it fair or ethical that the individual must sit through an attempt to convert them religiously? The answer to this could hinge on how forthcoming the leagues and participants are about their overall goals of proselytizing. Furthermore, does proselytizing masked as sports spectating corrupt sports' essence? If sports are essentially about competition and human skill improvement, does this co-opt or even appropriate sports? This unfolds even deeper questions about who owns or regulates sports. Does anyone or any entity actually own sports or are sports part of a cultural commonwealth available to all who would choose to play or with the ability to participate? Is this an example of sports *in* a religious tradition or sports appropriated *by* a religious tradition? This distinction could determine one's attitude toward the practice of sports proselytizing.

The second example of Jewish athletes playing sports as a cultural integration tool might appear more ethical. Any member of a society facing marginalization or stereotyping should use whatever resources at their disposal to improve their social standing, right? The means justifies the ends. However, what if these athletes carry undue stress to not simply win the game but succeed for their ethnic or religious ingroup? Is it fair to place this type of burden on athletes even if they volunteer to do so? What if an athlete chooses not to carry this responsibility and simply compete as an athlete? Upon immigrating, individuals develop differing perspectives of what immigration looks like and how much of their previous heritage they should maintain. Yet, some expect members of their religious or ethnic group to strive for better conditions for all members of the ingroup. If they chose not to champion their ingroup, they might receive backlash from their ingroup and criticism from others who suppose they should champion a bigger cause than winning.

Although members in each example might hold sincere intentions and motivations for how sports advance their current status, questions revolve around the usage of sports by religious communities. Assessing individual motivations and sincerity is a difficult task for any researcher; however, a strong interrogation of the power dynamics at play in specific situations results in a better understanding of how social positions inform certain moves and developments. Keep in mind that in some contexts certain groups experience exclusionary social and legal practices. The ingroup and outgroup structure is intended for one group to maintain control and privilege over another. Religions and sports are not immune to the ingroup/outgroup design and the manifesting power inherent in that design.

CHAPTER SYNOPSIS

This chapter investigates how some religious communities adopt and utilize sports for their benefit. In the first case study, some Christians adapt sports as a proselytizing tool to meet their need for sharing their religion with others. In these cases, sports become one outlet for some within Christianity to advance and recruit new members. To be clear, Christianity is not homogeneous, and not all Christians use sports in this way. The second illustration analyzes how some Jewish people participate in sports to gain social acceptance and learn more about the newly-immigrated society. These instances demonstrate the social and cultural capital gained from playing sports, and how sports supply a means to break down some ingroup/outgroup dynamics. Although only two examples, they provide a small sampling of how some religious communities utilize sports for objectives beyond mere competition or game play. Instead, sports, as cultural phenomena, allow an interaction with the broader society. As religious communities identify their agendas or social challenges, sports provide one possible solution for meeting religious communities' identified needs. Sports then are part of a cultural commonwealth available and accessible for most to engage.

Religious traditions constitute a toolbox of resources for adherents. Religious traditions include several resources like rituals, practices, and myths for adherents. These tools are dynamic, being shaped by the members as needed. If an old practice fails to meet the needs of the community, the practice can be modified, adapted, or abandoned. Religions are dynamic human activities. New tools also can be integrated into the religious tradition's toolbox like aspects of sports, games, and play. This enhances some religious communities' ability to accomplish their goals whether that be proselytizing, assimilation, or other objectives. In sum, sports are sometimes adapted as an instrument in the religious community's toolbox.

RECOMMENDED READING

Those trained as historians most commonly conduct research similar to the "sports in religions" approach. Numerous scholarly accounts of religious communities adopting sports exist. Timothy Chandler and Tara Magdalinski's *With God on Their Side: Sport in the Service of Religion* (2002) analyzes several global examples of sports being employed by religious groups to further their objectives. Linda Borish's study of Jewish women and sports participation, referenced in this chapter, situates nicely in this collection with examples of Catholic, Muslim, and Shinto case studies. As it pertains particularly to Jewish people's involvement in sports, Raanan Rein and David Sheinin's *Muscling in on New Worlds* (2014) supplies historical accounts from across North, Central, and South America. In each of these cases, the authors give special attention to how Jewish people helped mold the creation of new societies through sports and athleticism. A complementary book, Michael Brenner and Gideon Reuveni's *Emancipation Through Muscles: Jews and Sports in Europe* (2006), focuses on the European context with similar goals. Both of these collections contain contributions from various scholars from across the globe. Raanan Rein's *Fútbol, Jews, and the Making of Argentina* (2014) wonderfully analyzes the development of a Jewish soccer club, Club Atlético Atlanta, in Buenos Aires, and how this club aided in Jewish assimilation in Argentina.

Within Christian studies, scholars explore the role of "muscular Christianity" within Christian sporting participation. Muscular Christianity sought to develop brave, courageous, and athletically-trained men who would challenge the notion that religious men were effeminate. Clifford Putney's (2003) historiography, *Muscular Christianity: Manhood and Sports in Protestant America, 1880–1920*, shows how this philosophy took hold in the midst of urbanization and industrialization, and a general trend away from agricultural life. John Macaloon's *Muscular Christianity and the Colonial and Post-Colonial World* (2013) consists of a collection of chapters detailing the connections between colonial expansion and muscular Christian ideology. It provides a global perspective on this topic.

SPORTS AS RELIGIONS

The previous two chapters investigated the relationship of religions and sports from a distinct category perspective looking at how these phenomena intersect. Religious expressions can find their way into sporting spaces, and religious communities can adopt sports to further their objectives. The numerous examples given illustrate that there are no strict cultural boundaries between religions and sports. As the human world is full of various types of activities, it is easy to imagine numerous cultural phenomena interacting similarly. For example, we could imagine religious expressions entering into business corporations. Although a specific corporation might not be religious, some employees could conceivably carry religious commitments into workspaces. Often, there are protocols established to regulate these expressions and minimize discrimination and extend freedoms. Likewise, some businesses might participate in local sporting leagues to cultivate camaraderie amongst their employees. In short, there are no rigid lines demarcating where cultural expressions begin or end.

Transitioning the assessment from distinctive categories (religions and sports) to overlapping or mirroring phenomena moves the discussion to deeper considerations. More specifically, once we set aside the understanding that cultural phenomena can or should be compartmentalized, we can begin to see how human activities operate similarly or mirror one another. For example, thinking of religions as culturally integrative instead of uniquely distinctive helps us to recognize more fully the economic aspect of religions. Religious institutions typically need

DOI: 10.4324/9781003362630-4

financial funding to operate. Thus, thinking of religion as separate from economics limits a complete understanding of religions. Or, as another illustration, consider sports as a political act. There might be initial resistance to this proposition, with some claiming sports are apolitical, but the athletes playing games are also citizens or members of nations facing social issues. People maneuver through multiple domains of life every day. Think about how many different types of spaces you've entered in the last week or month. People circulate through educational, political, entertainment, religious, sporting, and familial spaces without giving much thought to the types of domains.

In this chapter, we set aside the idea that sports and religions are separate. This route positions us to consider if sports are a religion or not. Fortunately, there is plenty of material for us to examine. These arguments tend to posit sports as a universal and sacred part of human activity or that sports mirror religions in what they supply their human participants. Coming to terms with the "sports as religions" position often takes time, and there could be initial resistance to some of these proposals. One way to think about this is mere overlap in functionality: religions and sports function similarly. This position argues that sports provide ritual opportunities, identity commitments, and establishing outlets for human energies, much like religions supply. To visually represent this, see the adjustment from our previous models depicted in Figure 4.1.

This doesn't necessarily mean that sports fulfill *each and every* function that religions do; instead, sports offer some of the

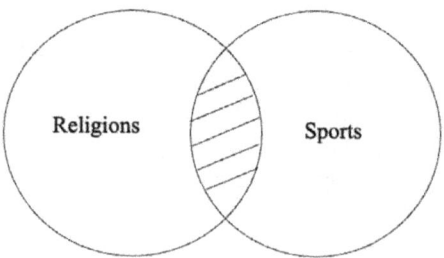

Figure 4.1

same fulfillments of needs and desires that religions provide. This might seem controversial to some, but to others this position might not extend the argument far enough. Instead, some sports fans and athletes might contend that there isn't mere overlap between religions and sports but a shared essence. In this case, sports are religious, providing a space of devotion and forming a purpose for human life. Just as some people commit their entire life to a deity or religious community, some sports fans and athletes devote themselves to their games and teams. Sports, from this position, should be listed alongside other religious traditions like Buddhism, Jainism, and Christianity. Figure 4.2 attempts to convey this overlapping.

In brief, the arguments proposing that sports are religious primarily center on two approaches: sports are sacred human activities or sports are functionally religious. These approaches share several similarities while also both being unique. In the following, we will review these approaches and some of the primary voices favoring these theories. Getting into the details of these arguments (highlighting which sports are recognized as religious and in what ways) unravels the complexity of the claims. As a means of demonstrating how sports get theorized as religious activities, we first explore a case study involving the sport of pickleball. As pickleball is an emerging sport and some are unfamiliar with it, I spend some time detailing the development of pickleball and its rules. Once we review this case study, I apply

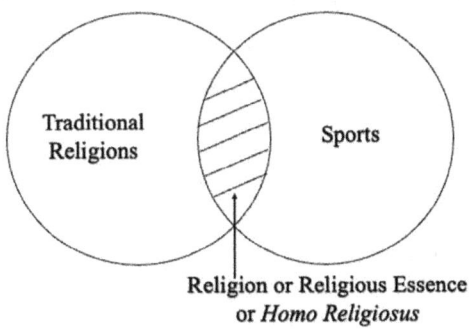

Figure 4.2

theoretical frameworks from scholar Mircea Eliade. This application shows how theories designed specifically for traditional forms of religious expressions can be applied to sporting phenomena. Several other sports with longer histories, like baseball, soccer, and football, are typically the focus of scholars applying religious theories; however, using pickleball demonstrates how quickly the backstories and places of sports can be sacralized. Reviewing other scholarly examples leads to a discussion centering on the essence of human nature. Ultimately, the goal is to demonstrate how arguments are made that position sports as religion and what this means for understanding human life. Once these assertions are summarized, I then offer some counter arguments for deliberation. The point is not to settle this conversation once and for all but to open a robust discussion around this topic.

> **BOX 4.1 INITIAL THOUGHTS**
>
> The opening of this chapter might take some people by surprise. How can sports be comparable to religious devotion, commitments, and practice? People landing on either side of this debate could take offense to the notion that sports are religious activities. From one perspective, some sports fans might be very skeptical of the idea that they are religiously devoted to their sports teams or sports. Especially if someone finds the concept of religious devotion troublesome, they might find the proposition of sports as religions insulting. They might argue, "I am a sports fan, but not religious." In a similar but opposing perspective, a religiously devout person who spends their resources, time, and energies in devotion to a deity or religious community could believe sports is a lesser human activity compared to religious devotion. Sports are for fun or play, not serious enough to be considered religious. They could pronounce, "Sports are not religious. This mocks my religious devotion." The argument is quite problematic for those who are sincerely committed to their sports or religions.
>
> If you are initially suspicious of this idea, take consolation in the knowledge that numerous people I speak with have the same immediate reaction, even if they aren't necessarily offended. One time a very kind woman asked me what I taught at my university

during an intermission of a theater production. When I replied I taught religions and sports, her response was, "I guess they'll teach anything these days." Embedded in this sarcastic response is a skepticism that sports and religions could possibly have anything in common. Her apprehension is rooted in her assumptions about religions and sports, and this returns us to human categorical ways of thinking and to how definitions of sports and religions frame our understandings.

Let me stress: it is fine to maintain reluctance about sports as religious expression, but we need to examine why we have such apprehension about this proposition in the first place. In this section, the following two reflection exercises have the reader assess, as much as possible, their assumptions regarding sports as religions. Feel free to complete one or both of the exercises.

> Exercise 1: Without consulting any resources, take time to write down a working definition of religion. A prompt I often give my students is to consider this: An alien life form is visiting planet Earth. Your task is to explain religion to this life form that has no idea about human culture or phenomena. You only have two to three sentences available for explanation. How do you define religions universally, so the alien life form has an adequate understanding?
>
> As you jot this down, remember some of the early material discussed in the first chapter of this book. If the definition requires deities or a deity, then the definition might be too narrow to include some nontheistic forms of Buddhism and Jainism. And if your definition only includes one deity, then you've restricted many polytheistic traditions from the idea of religion. How, at all, can religion be defined to encapsulate all religious traditions?
>
> After forming your definition, review it and consider if sports meet the parameters of the definition. For instance, if the definition includes practices and beliefs about how life should be lived, then sports could easily fit into the parameters since there are rules and morals attached to sports and rituals embedded in sports (as we will see later in the chapter). Maybe take time to discuss this with others. Can others help you see how sports might fit into your definition of religion?

> Exercise 2: Make a list, from your vantage point, of the ways sports do and do not fit into a religion category. Using two columns, compose a pros and cons list for the proposition "sports are religions," remembering that there are numerous varieties within sports and religions. Consider the various components of religions and sports as the columns are composed. What are the shared characteristics listed? Are these enough to support the proposition that sports are religious activity? Or are there drastic differences in the columns verifying the distinction between the two phenomena? Ask a friend, classmate, or coworker to help you to gain different input into this discussion. When finished, compare the columns.

SPORTS AS RELIGIONS

Every sport has an origin and stories around the origin, and the sport of pickleball is no different. Across the Puget Sound from Seattle, Washington, lies Bainbridge Island. This island is a short, approximately 30-minute, ferry ride from Seattle, a bustling seaport city and the largest major city in the Pacific Northwest of the continental United States. Bainbridge Island hosts numerous tourists and people living in the Seattle-Tacoma area during the drier summer months. During the summer of 1965, a couple of vacationing families developed a new game, which they would later call pickleball, to keep themselves entertained. The game of pickleball, although slow to take off as a sport, has now developed into a growing sport with millions of players in the United States and new leagues emerging globally. The game has become so popular that there are pickleball-themed weddings and celebrity participants. New professional leagues, cross-country tournaments, and corporate competitions are attempting to capitalize on the sport's growing popularity. In March 2022, the governor of Washington, Jay Inslee, even made pickleball the state sport of Washington.

The game of pickleball mixes tennis, ping pong, and badminton. Players utilize a court smaller than a standard tennis court, paddles, and a wiffle ball, with a net similar to that found on tennis courts, and the game is won by reaching 11 points. Although there are singles formats, most pickleball players compete in a two versus two format, allowing four players to play on one court at once. Over the years, paddle technologies have developed leading to players experimenting with spins, hard slices, and strategic positioning of the ball. Teams can only score if they serve the ball, and the serve must be hit underhanded.

On Bainbridge Island, pickleball courts carry a particular kind of significance. Island residents worked hard to fundraise and install pickleball courts at the local Battle Point Park, which they call "Founders Courts." Founders Courts include historical markers detailing the history of the game on the island. Currently including six courts, these pickleball courts host dozens of players on most days, unless the weather makes play impossible. Additionally, residents preserved the original badminton court where Joel Pritchard, Bill Bell, and Barney McCallum created the game. This site, known as Court One, is nestled in a backyard down the road from Battle Point Park.

Analyzing the activities surrounding the original site, the Founders Courts, and an annual tournament on Bainbridge Island reveals some interesting parallels with religious expressions. Each year, Bainbridge Island hosts an annual tournament attracting players from the Puget Sound area. The tournament brackets vary depending on skill level and age of the participants. More recently, pickleball enthusiasts have begun traveling to the island to play on the original site as the sport gains momentum. Players who come to the tournament join in to attempt to win their age and skill division at Founders Courts, but some also take a trip to Court One and hit a few balls to claim they've played on the first pickleball court. Moreover, the tournament begins with a wooden paddle tournament mimicking the earliest stages of the sport's development. Very few people play with the early, wooden version of the pickleball paddle; today paddles vary widely, but most are a composite of lightweight materials like aluminum and graphite.

When I spoke with local residents who led the pickleball preservation efforts, many were proud of their work and were happy to see players traveling to visit the island. Yet, there was another key element of the game they were determined to preserve: the fun-loving, inviting ethos surrounding the game of pickleball. The original game was created to bridge generational divides, and rules were established to keep players from simply standing at the net and slamming the ball on the opposing team: a small area divides opposing team members by building a "kitchen," or non-volley zone, near the net. Pickleball players on Bainbridge Island proclaim the sport open and available for all to participate in. The rules also establish that teams get to determine if the ball is out of bounds on their side of the court. This practice creates a game of trust wherein teams should play the game fairly. If one team cannot make an out-of-bounds call, they look to the other team for assistance in making the call.

The continued efforts to preserve and re-enact aspects of pickleball's development and history corresponds with Mircea Eliade's theories regarding religious rituals. Eliade, a Romanian scholar, was interested in human rituals around re-creating myths and events and how these religious rituals contribute to human meaning making. In his work, *The Sacred and the Profane* (1959), he argued that ancient people designated certain days and periods as more meaningful than others. These days included rituals and rites to imbue life with meaning and connect ritual participants with the past. Baptisms and other ceremonies provide a means of moving through phases of life – think from childhood into adulthood – and join the ritual participant with previous generations of practitioners. This joining of the present with the past establishes a certainty regarding how life should be lived, builds an identity based on historical association, and affirms the individual's participation. These events are typically centered on myths regarding the formation of the cosmos or the people group (tribe, community, etc.) and recreate events. Eliade argued, "every religious festival, any liturgical time, represents the actualization of a sacred event that took place in a mythical past, 'in the beginning'" (pp. 68–69). By connecting with a mythical past, humans create purpose in life. Think of Muslims who participate in the Hajj, which mimics the Prophet Muhammed's footsteps and actions, or Jewish people remembering the liberation of early Jewish people from Egyptian rule through the Passover Seder. These rituals make it all real to those within these traditions.

Applying Eliade's theory of sacralizing events to pickleball, the wooden paddle tournament re-performs the sport's earliest days. Although few play with a wooden paddle today, using the wooden paddle connects players with a bygone era. This recreation connects players with the founders and the earliest innovators of the game. Playing on Founders Courts builds another meaning-making layer. Although there are thousands of pickleball courts across the globe, Founders Courts attaches players to the game's origins. To play on Bainbridge Island positions players at the *axis mundi* (the center of the world) of the pickleball world. Then some players make a pilgrimage visit to Court One, a mythic re-connecting to where it all began. The founding of pickleball is made real through playing in the annual Founders Tournament on Bainbridge Island. Moreover, the re-creation of the early pickleball and pilgrimage to the origin site reaffirms the ethos that locals proclaim. If the earliest players simply wanted to have fun with an interactive game, then current players are reminded of what the essence of the sport is. Taken altogether, the wooden paddle, touring Court One, and playing at Founders Courts permits the pickleball player to connect the past with the present with a future-looking objective of giving the game of pickleball to future generations. Time – past, present, and future – interconnect for the participant, making pickleball a game transcending normal, mundane life.

As the game of pickleball explodes competitively with financial backing and new market shares surrounding it, local pickleball residents on Bainbridge Island concern themselves with sharing the original ethos and purpose of the game with others. The pickleball rituals on Bainbridge Island create a community of energized locals sharing the sport with others. In fact, pickleball ambassadors, a designation for some locals on the island, meet with pickleball enthusiasts visiting the island. These ambassadors lead tours to Court One and Founders Court and serve as a type of pickleball evangelist, proclaiming the good news of pickleball on the island and elsewhere. This forms a community of pickleball players that feed off each other's energies and commitments to preserving the game's authenticity.

This case study of pickleball is merely one example of how a scholar could apply theories of religion to sports. There are plenty of other examples. Onaje X.O. Woodbine (2016) applies theories of lived religion – religious expressions in the everyday apart from organized religious institutions – to argue the religiosity of inner-city basketball in Boston, Massachusetts. His work demonstrates how playing basketball ritualizes the memory of loss, hope, and healing for young men of color. Woodbine discovered a transcendent aspect to basketball: "This dimension on the court [of basketball] is fundamentally 'other' in nature, in that it gives expression to a mode of experience that goes beyond words, is ineffable, and involves the spectral presence of the dead" (p. 14). In essence, the game of basketball, played in various tournaments and public courts in Boston, creates the conditions where players experience "an urban 'lived religion'...expressed through rhythms, sounds, styles, symbols, transcendent experiences, and rituals" (p. 167). According to Woodbine, this religiosity exists beyond the walls of a church, mosque, or temple, but acts as religiosity for those playing the game.

Another case study is the example of a soccer (football) club in Argentina, which Eloísa Martín (2018) argues contains "gestures, practices, and meanings...used to create and experience the sacred" (p. 65). During Martín's fieldwork in South America, he noticed a complex matrix of symbols, fandoms, and rituals operating not as a "metaphor for religiosity" but as "practices of the sacred" (p. 65). Focusing on one soccer club that adopted a deceased local singer as their representative saint, the study highlights how soccer forms an opportunity for people to explore the sacred outside of traditional forms of religious institutions. Martín postulates that the soccer club forms an instructional collective guiding members into how to live life.

As seen in the examples, there are various approaches to understanding sports as a religious expression in the world. Sports are a type of independent religiosity separate from other religious traditions. From this perspective, sports are a religion alongside Buddhism, Islam, Christianity, etc. Many sports contain rich histories with icons and legends much like traditional religions. Religions then are about sacred exploration by humans and what channels humans use to reach what is sacred.

While some seek an experience with a transcendent deity, others seek the sacred in the mystery of a sporting outcome, commitment to a team or game, or devotion to pushing one's bodily limits within a sport. Furthermore, taking the position that sports are religious expressions in the world typically requires a corresponding position that humans are *homo religiosus*, or inherently religious. From this vantage point, humans are drawn to the sacred, otherworldly, or transcendent beyond the mundane. The mundane or profane is a means of identifying the ordinary, specifically in a move to distinguish that which is beyond the ordinary – the extraordinary. Some traditional religions codify how members or individuals may reach the sacred. This argument supposes aspects of human life as imbued with more meaning than other elements of life. For instance, the pickleball example highlights one element of life on Bainbridge Island that creates an opportunity for some residents to explore life beyond the mundane. There is something distinctively special about the game. Similarly, Woodbine and Martín's examples demonstrate spaces, events, and collectives supplying sacrality to a profane existence. This opens the topic of what is religious or sacred to potentially include any number of activities or phenomena, including movie watching, concert experiences, or spending time in natural environments like hiking. In sum, from these perspectives, sports are religious because they provide humans with a way to explore sacredness in the world.

If humans are *homo religiosus*, then a key element of human existence is the need for an outlet for religious expression. In more economically-developed countries, there is a decline in those affiliating with religions and participating in religious communities. Religious disaffiliation is part of a secularizing process of these societies, wherein people either have other obligations (i.e., economics) or their needs are comfortably met and, thus, they rely less on religious institutions. Although people in these societies depend less on religious institutions, if humans are *homo religiosus*, they would maintain religious needs. Sports are one available option to find a religious outlet – whether these people would claim such doesn't necessarily matter. Holding the *homo religiosus* position opens the conversation for what constitutes religion, even in the case of data showing people are less traditionally religious.

BOX 4.2 HOMO LUDENS

Digging deeper into the essence of sports and religions, one Dutch historian argues that play is the defining feature of being human. Studying cultural development across the globe, Johan Huizinga came to the conclusion that humans are *homo ludens* (which means that humans are playful creatures). Within his study, he defines play as:

> A free activity standing quite consciously outside "ordinary" life as being "not serious," but at the same time absorbing the player intensely and utterly. It is an activity connected with no material interest, and no profit can be gained by it. It proceeds within its own proper boundaries of time and space according to fixed rules and in an orderly manner. It promotes the formation of social groupings which tend to surround themselves with secrecy and to stress their difference from the common world by disguise or other means.
>
> (2016, p. 13)

This definition hinges on play being an aspect of life that is essential for the development of other cultural pursuits. Play consumes individuals, although there is no financial gain; instead, play forms collectives who differentiate themselves from others. He further states, "in play there is something 'at play' which transcends the immediate needs of life and imparts meaning to the action" (p. 1). Play is essential to human development, according to Huizinga.

Many associate play with children or child-like behavior, which links to Huizinga's emphasis on "not serious." Children typically love to play. Children enjoy playful fun, whether on playgrounds, with toys, or simply making up stories. Adults tend to remember when they played more as a child. This might have included building forts to defeat imaginary enemies, little leagues of baseball, soccer, or volleyball, or board games like Chutes and Ladders. However, life's responsibilities reduce the time some adults have to commit to playing. In these cases, these adults set aside their playful tendencies for the more serious business of financial attainment, family rearing, or career advancement. Due to this, play often is considered childish or irresponsible.

Play forms the essence of sports. Although professional and organizational sports embed financial objectives, they hinge on playing while taking play into a realm of seriousness. Samuel Duncan, a sports scholar, argues that this is problematic: "the problem with modern sport is that while play can indeed be serious, structured and disciplined it has become so serious, structured and disciplined that it has corrupted notions of fun, freedom, flair, spontaneity and creativity" (Duncan 2022, p. 282). Likewise, Duncan posits that professionalizing sports removes an essence of play. During play, "humans were able to be their whole self, which was essential for individuals to reach their full potential" (p. 285). It is the playfulness of sports that attracts human attention. For Huizinga, play is universal: "All peoples play, and play remarkably alike..." (2016, p. 28). This could be visualized as such in Figure 4.3.

Play, according to Huizinga, is more than the foundation of sports. Play is universal and the foundation of culture. Playing creates arts, literature, and other key elements of human society. As humans play with elements, art and stories emerge. Similarly, play develops cultural rituals. Some religious rituals and practices could owe their origins to play. While humans participate in play, new myths of deities, cosmological construction, and legends unfold. It might be difficult to think of religions as playful since many people take religious commitments very seriously today, but imagine the earliest development of these stories as humans played with plots, characters, and twists in the stories.

Huizinga's hypothesis that proposes play as fundamental could reverse our earlier proposition of sports as religions; instead, we

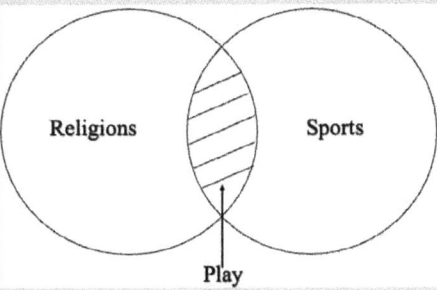

Figure 4.3

could understand some parts of religious practices as a kind of playfulness. Immediately, one might consider members of religious traditions as team members with a sporting objective to win an overarching human competition. However, let's analogize religions to playfulness with an example of future prediction and textual decoding. Many religious traditions contain texts that some members attempt to decipher. Whether this is decoding certain symbols like in the Christian text of Revelation or the Jewish Kabbalists who mystically seek to decipher Jewish writings, textual deciphering enacts a type of play. In these examples, specific references are said to represent larger (and more contemporary) persons, places, and events. Some people write these predictive renderings off as marginal within the traditions. Looking closer at these more mystical adaptations of the traditions, we can see the playfulness embedded within these activities: these practices stretch the human imagination using the resources supplied within the tradition.

Without being disrespectful to religious adherents, we could imagine the stories about deities as originally a playful way to engage the human imagination and to entertain. African folklore tells of Huveane, who created the earth and humans. As he was relaxing and enjoying his creation, humans figured out sexual activity and became quite loud during their exploration of this new activity. The noise of humans engaging in sex drove Huveane to build a ladder to the heavens so he could escape the noisy humans. Likewise, Greek and Roman myths recount numerous stories about the problematic situations involved in being a god or goddess and their relation to humans. Demeter punished an overly greedy human, Erysichthon, by giving him an unquenchable appetite. Once Erysichthon consumes everything he can get his hands on, he eventually turns to eating his own flesh. Through playful creation, these stories transmit cultural morals and ethics.

As a thought experiment, consider where play might be discovered, even if subversively. What other cultural components are forms of play or playfulness? Think about the earliest emergence of these components and how they might have developed from playful imagination. Additionally, how else can religions be considered forms of human play or sport? What stories, rituals, or practices are actually playful (but maybe carry a serious form today)?

FUNCTIONALLY SACRED AND SECULARIZATION

Another approach taken by scholars proposing sports are religious is dependent on the secularization thesis. The secularization thesis posits that as scientific reasoning, human advancements, and comforts increase for people, people will inevitably become less religious and eventually be completely independent from religious thought. Religions, in this sense, are recognized as essential but antiquated aspects of human development. Humans lacked answers to questions, and religious thought temporarily filled the gap by providing all types of responses. This includes questions regarding life and death, the universe and planetary development, and catastrophes. Now that science supplies answers to human questions that religions attempted to answer historically, people are generally less reliant on religious resources.

Yet it's not simply that religions supplied answers, but those religions fulfilled (or slowly developed) some human needs and desires. For instance, science might explain that burning incense contains no magical ability to change reality, but this might not stop some individuals from trying. Religions perform certain functions for humans; in this case, incense burning functions as an attempt to alter the ways things are. Knowing there is an increase in some countries in people disaffiliating with and committing less to religious institutions, some functions might still need satisfying. This is where some scholars argue sports enter the equation. "Human drives and needs that compel some to be a part of a particular religion are the same drives and needs that compel some to be a part of sport in some way…Sport can function like a religion in that it meets the same needs and desires satisfied or promised by formal religions," argue religious studies scholars Eric Bain-Selbo and Gregory Sapp (2016, p. 2). Although not all concur with this proposition (Higgs and Braswell 2004), the functionalist approach proposes that sports are displacing religions in meeting certain functional needs.

One of the ways religions functioned in the past was to establish a rhythm to human life. Each religious tradition consists of numerous holy days, special occasions, and ritual events marking specific moments in life or the calendar year. The Christian tradition certainly offers individuals and communities a rhythmic pattern of life. For individuals, life is marked with baptism, catechism (or something similar), and death rituals. These rituals signify admittance into the community, purpose in life, and, eventually, recognition in death. There are seasonal holy days for the Christian community like Lent, Easter, Advent, and Christmas. These celebrations align with seasonal changes like the beginnings of spring and winter. In Christian communities, different colors represent the calendrical periods with visual symbols. The holy days signaled religious events but also pragmatic functions for planting, harvesting, and resting. Similar rhythms are found in other religious traditions as well.

Like religious seasonal patterns, sports functionally offer a rhythm of life for its participants. In his book, *From Season to Season*, Joseph L. Price (2001) postulates that baseball is a functional annual calendar similar to religions. Known as America's "pastime," the baseball season emerges in the spring with a training period when the grass begins to green from the winter cold. At this time, baseball fans emerge from indoor seclusion to gather with others, eagerly evaluating the strengths and weaknesses of their teams. Opening Day is celebrated with numerous games, celebrations, and opening pitches from U.S. presidents, but it also carries with it a mythic dimension. According to Price, "Opening Day of Major League Baseball is most important because of its timing in spring (the time of planting), a time that coincides with nature's new year and corresponding celebrations of fertility rites" (p. 54). The season wraps up with a World Series taking place in late October and November, when colder weather shuts down outdoor play. In this instance, baseball displaces the necessity of a traditional religious calendar of events due to a secularizing society. Price argues, "the primary function of the American sports calendar is to provide some kind of ritual transition from the chaos of secularity to the cosmos of sports, from cultural malaise to corporate hope" (p. 57). Like other sports, baseball establishes a subversive reference on time – alignment with seasonal changes, ways to track chronological progress, and human movement.

The position that sports function like religions does not have to extend to sports are religions. The latter proposition equates the phenomena; the former positions the two phenomena as mirroring or similar, not necessarily equivalent. Whereas Price argues that baseball displaces religions, Jeffrey Scholes and Raphael Sassower (2014) detail several similarities between sports and religions without necessarily equating the two. Since sports and religions are both human creative ventures, it only makes sense that commonalities would emerge. One of the interesting examples they explicate is on the topic of relics. Relics are material objects granted historical significance by some people serving the "general function of carrying meaning that supersedes its mere materiality" (p. 77). These objects connect individuals to historical persons, events, or texts.

Like religious relics, sports involve several material objects granted increased significance. This includes balls, bats, racquets, uniforms, equipment, etc., that are involved with record breaking, championship winning, or specific players. Keeping with the sport of baseball, Scholes and Sassower review the case of a baseball relic involving the Chicago Cubs and fan, Steve Bartman. To make a long story short, Bartman interfered with a foul ball catch during the 2003 baseball playoffs, potentially costing the Cubs the opportunity to advance to the World Series. Fans immediately harassed Bartman (he even received death threats), and the actual baseball became a "despised, but special relic that absorbed the anger of fans and players alike" (p. 76). Eventually, the ball was bought and destroyed in a public ceremony to ritually appease the baseball gods. In this scenario, a material object (an infamous baseball) carried years of athletes' and fans' anger, frustration, and failure. These emotions, symbolized in the baseball, were then soothed with a public ritualized destruction of the ball. This baseball ritual mimicked religious rituals.

In secularizing societies, the remnants of religious expressions still visibly remain, suggesting sports as religions or sports *functioning* as religious expression. Even though people might abandon religious affiliations and commitments to religious institutions, humans retain certain needs and must find ways to fulfill those needs. Sports step in where religion is abandoned. It is difficult in these instances to know if these needs and fulfillment of these needs are religious in nature or religious-like. In other words, are humans *homo religiosus* making sports religious or is this simply the next step in human development, making sports a step past religions?

BOX 4.3 SACRED SEARCHES, MOVIES, AND DISENCHANTMENT

Most people would agree with the notion that there are sacred (or special) aspects of life distinguishable from the more profane (or mundane) aspects. For some, work is a mundane aspect of life required in many capitalist-driven societies. This mundanity is depicted in movies like *Joe Versus the Volcano* and *Office Space*. The lead characters begrudgingly trudge through their office hours and perceive their work life as an anchor holding them from really experiencing life. In each of these movies, the lead characters can break out of the monotonous patterns of their life through changing their routine and experiencing something new or making different choices in their daily operations. *The Secret Life of Walter Mitty* wonderfully depicts the breaking of typical daily patterns. In that film, Walter Mitty, played by Ben Stiller, initially finds hope in his daydreaming of what he wishes life to be instead of his tasks of developing photographic film for pictures in *Time* magazine. Eventually, prompted by his need to find a lost photo, Mitty goes on a grand adventure leading him across the globe. During this time, Mitty experiences life on a different plane. He rides a skateboard down a mountainside in Iceland, jumps from a helicopter into shark-infested waters, and eventually finds his objective in the Himalayan mountains, where he gets to lay eyes on a snow leopard. In sum, these films both portray work life as crippling, and also the possibility to break free from the monotony of office life.

These films resonate with many people. One scholar, Max Weber, diagnosed dissatisfaction with modern life as disenchantment. Although modernity provides comforts – i.e., air conditioning, medical treatments, and quick modes of transportation – Weber speculated that something was still missing from modern life in more developed countries. In his book, *The Protestant Ethic and the Spirit of Capitalism* (1930), he ties the emergence of capitalism to embedded Protestant ideas. Weber thought that the fusion of Protestant thought and capitalism formed an intense need to labor diligently, save money, and continually increase material production. He used the metaphor of modern people living in capitalist-driven societies as stuck in an iron cage. He even predicted that this iron cage would continue to exist until all the fossil fuels had been extracted from the earth. This is a bleak picture of life, but Weber thought there was a profound disenchantment in residing in the modern, industrialized era. Part of the problem, he proposed, was that religion had attempted to be rationalized through the Protestant Reformation, and the mysterious was eliminated in how people understood their world.

Applying Weber's ideas, we can see all kinds of art forms and activities as attempting to reduce disenchantment or re-enchant the world. The aforementioned films portray disenchantment with life: life is scheduled and routine, and there seems to be no way out of routinized life. However, each of the main characters can find something special or sacred about the human experience. This fundamentally shows a pervasive notion of a sacred (not necessarily *the* sacred) that can be located if a search commences. Far from a nihilistic view, wherein all of life is meaningless, these portrayals demonstrate the notion that some of life is sacred while other aspects are simply mundane. Humans need to know when they are living in the profane or the sacred.

If humans, or at least most humans, are *homo religiosus* trying to find or pronounce meaning in certain events or elements of life, then we could begin to make a list of elements that are sacred and those that are profane. A fun exercise is trying to decide which parts of life fall into which category. This can be done by keeping a journal of activities over a day, week, or month. Which parts of life seem more meaningful? Why? Which parts of life appear profane or mundane? Why? An alternative approach would be to watch films focusing on sports. What do these films have in common? What role do sports or pursuing a sports championship have in movies? How are humans depicted in these plots?

If life can be categorized in this way, which tends to be a Western way of seeing the world, then we could also begin to find the relevancy in the arguments that sports are religious or sacred activities for some people. Whether this is from an athlete's or fan's perspective, sports could be indexed as religious or a type of religion in the same way that a member of a religious tradition might find meaning within that tradition.

SPORTS AS RELIGIONS, A COUNTER ARGUMENT

The sports as religions argument can be quite convincing. These arguments do make general connections between what humans consider sacred. Most of us know someone who is a sports fanatic, an extreme fan who is completely devoted to their team (s), clubs, or games. A student of mine once shared with me a private room at their grandparents' house, which was off-limits to all visitors. This room contained memorabilia from the New England Patriots, an NFL football team. In a photo she shared with me, there were jerseys from specific Patriots players framed and hanging on the walls, autographed footballs, and other trinkets carefully displayed around the small room. Even a small, wooden structure appeared to be an altar. The student swore she peeked into the room and saw her grandmother praying one Sunday morning at that little altar for the Patriots to win their game. When examples like these are presented, there seems to be little reason to doubt that sports are religious or religious-like devotion for some fans.

There are some counterarguments against the sports as religions position that should be considered. In this section, I present two criticisms against the proposition that sports are religions. First, you might remember from the first chapter that religion as a category has a long history of colonial projection. As a quick reminder, Western colonialists adopted a project to discover religion as they expanded their economic and territorial agendas. They tended to project religion onto cultural practices, ceremonies, or rituals in societies and cultures that had no corresponding idea of religion. Part of the identifying religion project agenda was to spread their religion, Christianity. As they attempted to Christianize, they inevitably religionized the globe. Foundationally, the assumption was that all humans are religious (*homo religiosus*). In other words, because they desperately wanted to find religion, they incorrectly discovered "religion" in places where it simply didn't exist.

Like the colonialist agenda to dominate and exploit cultures and their environmental resources, "discovering" religion in sports could be considered a continuation of the religionization project. Foundationally assuming that all humans contain religious needs that must be satisfied reifies the colonialist error. There is no actual hard evidence that determines that humans are universally *homo religiosus*. Additionally, many theories applied to sports as religion tend to privilege Abrahamic traditions (i.e., Judaism, Christianity, and Islam) as the standard bearer of what constitutes religion. A majority of the earlier theorists were Europeans, and they used Abrahamic traditions as the model for religion and then prescribed universal aspects of religion to other cultural traditions. To state that the pilgrimage to Court One on Bainbridge Island is a religious pilgrimage evokes Christian pilgrimages to the Holy Land or Muslim Hajj pilgrimages. Likewise, proclaiming basketball as a ritual site for transcendence or soccer as catechism works directly from Christian expressions. Most of the work from scholars arguing that sports are religious operates from these theoretical frameworks tied to Christianity. There is a chance that some sports are Christian expressions, but universally religious could be a stretch, or worse, a reworked, colonialist-like miscalculation.

Second, there is the argument that sports are religions is gendered and typically utilizes revenue-generating sports or games, which are inherently violent or contain a level of physical danger as primary examples. By gendered, I mean that most scholars arguing sports are religious are men *and* that most of their examples tend to be male-dominated sports. American football, international soccer, baseball, and basketball historically have been played more by men. There are certainly examples of women playing these sports, but the examples provided by most sports *as* religions proponents tend to ignore the participation of female athletes. This is certainly interesting since many recognized religions tend to be male dominated, but this also marginalizes half of the human population. Moreover, the violence instantiated within sports is often a key part of the religious argument. Woodbine's example is about the trauma suffered from inner city life and how basketball creates a transcendent space to work through suffering. Bain-Selbo (2009) utilizes the violence within American football as a key part of human and religious development. He argues,

> football was saved not by eliminating violence but by compromising on an acceptable degree of physical danger. Violence in this case would be... a rite of passage designed to usher young men into the rough-and-tumble world of adulthood.
>
> (p. 67)

To be clear, not all examples are inherently violent or risky, but, more often than not, violence and physical risk are involved in the arguments. These examples tend to assume that male bodies can truly know transcendence, and risks are a key element of this knowledge. This might inadvertently hint at how historical religious expressions codified risky elements championed from male experiences (and how this has eventually evolved to correspond with modern values). Recognizing the male experiences recorded within religious texts illustrates the overwhelming attention given historically to these accounts versus their female counterparts. Are religions based on male experience? Is this true historically, but not today?

Each of these counter arguments could be resolved, but they have yet to be. As theories develop and are applied to case studies, the case studies impress the need to tweak or modify the theory. These counter arguments call for more case studies beyond male-dominated sports and reconsidering the foundations of the subfield. Does women's volleyball function the same as American football? Or does tennis supply a space of transcendence? If so, what is being transcended? In short, is the sports as religions claim a male argument or attempt to justify the games, physical risks, and competitions embedded in male sports?

CHAPTER SYNOPSIS

This chapter reviews arguments positing sports are either (a) religious or (b) functionally religious. These two positions have a slight nuance, which is tremendously significant for application. If sports are religious, religious needs or desires are central to what it means to be human. These religious impulses need to be addressed. If sports function similarly to religious expressions, then fundamentally sports and religions are both human ventures and simply share characteristics. The former option could still be premised on a *homo religiosus* position. These two positions influence how research is conducted and theories applied. For example, if the pilgrimage on Bainbridge Island by pickleball players is religious, then the geographical area of the Pacific Northwest known for being the least traditionally religious in the United States requires reexamination. Religion simply looks different than we expect while still existing. If the pilgrimage to Court One and Founders Courts is *like* religion, then maybe some players simply think there is a specialness beyond the mundane in playing pickleball in this location. This slight difference impacts much of what is considered to be religion or how humans simply operate in the world.

Moreover, some critiques of the sports as religious position demonstrate the potential holes in the theories proclaimed primarily by male scholars. The gendered nature of the arguments tends to ignore female athletes and women's participation in sports. Many of the theories could hinge on disenchantment with the role of men in a modernized and industrialized world. The sports as religions argument might illustrate a male's desire to take physical risks and compete using their bodies, which is not necessarily a religion argument. These positions highlight the often-portrayed human desire to seek out excitement and break out of the monotony of everyday routines. Whether this says more about the structures of contemporary societies or human desires for the sacred needs further investigation.

RECOMMENDED READING

Chapters 2, 3, and 4 detail the most common scholarly frameworks for studying the relationships between religions and sports. Assessing which position a scholar embraces within their research is a valuable analytical exercise. Most scholars tend to be very clear about their approach, and several bring important nuances to the sports as religions discussion. In addition to the works referenced in this chapter, the following recommendations include books and academic journal articles that could be given a microscopic reading in order to examine the methodology and approach articulated by the authors. When reviewing these works consider whether the approach complements a "sports as religions" approach or one of the first two frameworks: sports in religions or religions in sports. Some potential books to consider include:

Playing with God: Religion and Modern Sport by William J. Baker (2007)
The Eternal Presence of Sport: Rethinking Sport and Religion by Daniel A. Grano (2017)
God in the Stadiums: Sports and Religion in America by Robert J. Higgs (1995)
On the 8th Day: A Catholic Theology of Sport by Matt Hoven, J.J. Carney, and Max T. Engel (2022)
Of God and Games by William J. Baker (2016)
Godspeed: Racing is My Religion by L.D. Russell (2009)

Combined with these books, several academic journal articles explore whether sports are religious activities. The following articles are available in most university libraries and Google Scholar.

- "Hockey: A Divine Sport?," Tracy Trothen. 2006. *Studies in Religion*
- "Is the Comparison of Sport to Religion Justified?," Damian Barnat. 2019. *Studies in Sport Humanities*
- "Football, Conservative Values, and a Feeling of Oneness with the Group: A Study of Polish Football Fandom," Radosław Kossakowski and Tomasz Besta. 2018. *East European Politics and Societies and Cultures*
- "Cricket, Society and Religion: A Study of Increasing Religiosity in the National Cricket Team of Pakistan," Ali Khan. 2021. *Sport in Society*.

These works compose a very short list of possible readings. In fact, the listing is simply the tip of a massive iceberg of materials related to the study of religions and sports. An additional exercise is searching for material to add to this collection. Online libraries and Google Scholar are great places to begin this search. When searching, consider using the general terms "religion and sports" or specific religious traditions and sports like: Buddhism and basketball; Judaism and baseball; or Hinduism and cricket. What did you discover? How does the material align, challenge, or add to the three frameworks discussed thus far in the book?

RELIGIONS AND SPORTS IN DIALOGUE

In the preceding chapters, we focused attention on sports and religions as either a specific type of space or expression. In the former, sports and religions operate commonly in places designated for such activities. Whether it be at a mosque, church, or temple, like sporting fields, pitches, and courts, people build these venues for particular rituals or games. Yet, because humans are multidimensional, various types of expressions appear in these spaces. A religious expression might occur in a sporting space or a sports game might surface in a religious space. Sports and religions cross boundaries. Furthermore, sports and religions share similarities in their constitution. The two phenomena share analogous rituals, superstitions, icons, narratives, and other elements. Whether there are merely familial resemblances or sports and religions are of the same substance (as in sports are religious activities), sports and religions expressively mimic each other. We can confidently posit that at minimum sports and religions are relational in the sense that they look alike in certain instances.

Sports and religions, however, compose much more than expressions and spaces in the contemporary world. Each of these phenomena includes finances, develops relationships, and exerts social influence. In other words, sports and religions carry a social, financial, and political currency in societies across the globe. Many people still look to religious leaders, local and national, to give direction during difficult times in life or facilitate special occasions like weddings, births, and funerals. Also, with the advancement of social media, people listen to popular athletes and coaches for their

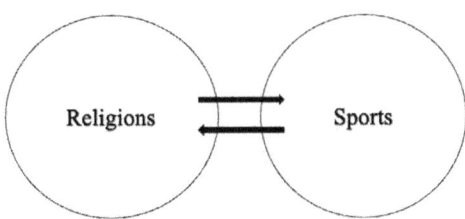

Figure 5.1

positions on political and social issues. On account of this influence, athletes and religious leaders sometimes have a dialogue on issues affecting societies. This is the fourth framework proposed by Forbes and Mahan (2017), and crudely represented in Figure 5.1. According to these authors, dialogue includes both when athletes and religious leaders "(a) talk to and about the other side, and (b) when they engage in conversation about issues in which they have a shared interest. The term 'dialogue' here is meant broadly, including affirmations, denunciations, observations, and shared concerns" (p. 20). Through various types of media, these discussions often are made public whether they are cooperative, combative, or somewhere in between. In this chapter, we attend to the messiness of human life, how religions and sports advocates articulate positions regarding social issues, and the relationship of sports and religious leaders in these matters. To begin, we take a moment to deglamorize sports and religions. As people hold sports and religions in high regard, we must be honest and discuss the uglier aspects of each. Then two case studies, using professional basketball as our sporting case study, demonstrate how dialogue between sports and religions occurs directly and indirectly. Some of the topics discussed in the subsequent sections carry an intellectual and emotional weight when compared to the topics discussed thus far in the book. Please be aware that, for some readers, these topics might be personal and spark some sensitive responses.

IMPERFECT HUMAN INSTITUTIONS

Thus far in this book, religions and sports are presented and analyzed primarily in a positive light. Sports get adopted by religious communities because sports and games are perceived as spaces that contribute to bringing out the best in individuals. Whether this be sports as a disciplining mechanism to develop work ethics or an opportunity to display one's best self, sports constitute a positive outlet. Likewise, when athletes express religiosity in a sporting space, some fans admire the athlete's dedication and devotion displayed in public. Fasting requires a dedication to complete – if an athlete fasts and participates in sports, it demonstrates their allegiance to their faith and athletic goals. Many of the scholarly voices included in the sports as religions arguments could be cast as sports and religions apologists (defenders of these phenomena). Sports and religions, as this argument proposes, are essential for humanity: they unite us, bring out the best in us, propel athletes and adherents to reach their maximum potential, and connect us with past humans who participated in similar rituals, events, and exercises. Based on my teaching experience, I would say most of my students think of most religions as a pure human activity intending to unite and bring peace into the world. Similarly, students find it difficult to critique sports because of their dedication to particular sports or teams. Certainly, some individuals question the glamorization of sports and religions, but, from my experiences, most people maintain that religions and sports instill qualities like unity, wholesome competition, and fairness. In order to offer a fair analysis of sports and religions, we must entertain the notion that sports and religions also exhibit negative qualities like divisiveness, violence, and inequality. The following paragraphs examine the darker side of sports and religions very briefly – but much more can be reviewed on these topics. My objective here is to acknowledge the imperfect aspects of sports and religious institutions while showing how these human ventures often reproduce negative social aspects.

Both religions and sports are usually painted as unifying human phenomena. Glossy images of large groups of people praying or meditating together or fans celebrating a hard-fought victory portray collectives setting aside differences, even if temporarily, to focus on shared objectives. These objectives might be in displaying a devotion to a supernatural being or revering a team's efforts in obtaining a championship; yet, unity often comes at the expense of a level of exclusion. The long history of conflicts between religious groups (e.g., Christian and Muslim, Protestant and Catholic, or Hindus and Sikhs) shows how religious groups often unify in a stance against another group. As stated in a previous chapter, sociologists and psychologists refer to this as ingroup/outgroup divisions or hierarchies. One person's identity formation can be based on an understanding of who they are in direct relation to a comparative other. At times, the comparative other is a person from competing religious traditions. A person in religious tradition X might establish their identity based on the rituals, codes, and practices of their tradition while also acknowledging their differences compared to religious tradition Y. Like race and ethnic divisions, sports can operate by separating groups of people against each other. Although some sports fans might maintain a level of respect for opposing teams' fans (because ultimately they are all football, soccer, or basketball fans), some fans sustain a deep hatred or animosity toward other teams. Additionally, sports, like religions, include a long history of excluding certain peoples. As journalists Jessica Luther and Kavitha Davidson (2020) note, "The world of sports has long been an exclusionary space, barring athletes of color and/or women and/or LGBTQ+ athletes from competing" (p. 1). Although sports and religions might unify people together around a common cause, let's not forget that unity can facilitate division. To be clear, not all religious traditions and sporting organizations encourage exclusionary practices or prescribe their members to engage in such attitudes and practices; however, establishing an ingroup inevitably results in creating outgroups.

Based on the divisions created through sports and religions, sometimes violence becomes instantiated in these phenomena. Several sporting examples could be cited. For instance, most are familiar with soccer fans engaging in violence during and after games. This rioting echoes historical episodes of soccer hooliganism where gangs of fans used racial slurs, fighting, and other disorderly behavior to intimidate opposing teams and fans. This type of violence is instantiated in most sports in various frequencies and degrees. On individual levels, coaches and athletes, endowed with respect and positions of power, sometimes abuse that power. Like some religious leaders, athletes and coaches perpetrate violence upon teammates and others (Owton and

Sparkes 2017; Parent et al. 2016). Helen Owton and Andrew Sparkes (2017) remind us that, "Various forms of abuse may be inflicted on young athletes who can be subjected to several forms of abuse at the same time, such as, physical abuse, sexual abuse, emotional abuse and neglect" (p. 732). Religious spaces can be sites of sexual abuse also (Raine and Kent 2019). The Catholic Church's sexual abuse scandals are well known, but cases of sexual abuse can be found in every tradition. Thus, the well-respected leaders in religious communities, athletes, and coaches can be guilty of engaging in illegal, illicit, or unethical behaviors. Numerous other examples could be detailed.

Beyond individual acts, sports and religions often reproduce social inequalities (Cooper et al. 2019). Baseball followed the segregationist policies within the United States for years. Basketball in the United States follows gender pay inequalities embedded in corporate America: WNBA players get paid much less than their male colleagues in the NBA. Although some might consider sports a meritocracy where individuals with the greatest talents rise to the top, income inequalities offer some wealthier individuals more opportunities than those in lower socio-economic statuses. With the advancement of medical enhancements, some athletes also adopt unfair advantages through steroids and human growth hormones. One group of scholars concludes, "sport is a site of entrenched inequalities along gender, race, nation and class lines" (Spaaij et al. 2015, p. 407). Religion operates in much the same way. Religious communities tend to reflect the social and class divisions of their society. Women and LBGTQ+ people, historically, have maintained a lower social status in religious traditions with patriarchy and heterosexuality advanced as normative. Sometimes sports and religions mirror social inequalities; at other times, these two institutions actually advocate for the inequalities as a correct social formation.

At a fundamental level, sports and religions are human activities infused with imperfect human qualities. Although both sports and religions give their devotees feelings of unity, peace, and equality, they also often incorporate disunity, violence, and inequality. This both/and approach reduces the glossiness often associated with both religions and sports; however, admitting the both/and positions the scholar to be more honest with assessments of cultural phenomena. Setting aside admiration and appreciation for sports and religions to conduct a more impartial examination shows the negative familial resemblances of sports and religions. Something to consider based on this assessment: are religions and sports unique human enterprises? Or stated differently, are sports and religions just similar to most of the cultural products humans engage with? Could we list fashion or business enterprises alongside religions and sports as deeply meaningful ventures granting some humans opportunities to invest their energies while also creating opportunities to deploy violence or unfair practices? These broad questions should make us consider if sports and religions are unique or not.

One thing that cannot be discounted is the social capital sports and religions maintain around the globe. Social capital reflects the influence and power these institutions have in various locations around the globe. This will obviously vary depending on location, but societies grant religious and sports leaders, along with their institutions, differing degrees of authority in speaking about assorted issues. As sports and religions are social and cultural institutions, they are positioned to respond to the unfavorable aspects of society.

BOX 5.1 SPORTS AND RELIGIOUS CONFLICTS

In their book, *Loving Sports When They Don't Love You Back*, journalists Jessica Luther and Kavitha Davidson (2020) accentuate numerous examples of the imperfect nature of sporting institutions. They argue, "Sports are big business, and with that comes the dirtiness of any major money making thing that holds cultural significance" (p. 1). Yet, they also admit: "Welcome to our club for sports fans who care too much. It's exhausting here, but we can't leave. We don't want to" (p. 1). This can create quite a conundrum for sports fans who love the game but simultaneously are repulsed by certain elements of the sports they love. Coupled with all the emotions of wins and losses, the community of fans, and energy involved in following a favorite athlete, sports often disappoint with exclusionary practices, negative connotations associated with mascots or logos, or athletes who conduct themselves in dishonorable ways.

By the same token, some religious people might feel conflicted about certain elements or teachings of their religious community. We should not assume individuals devoted to a religious community absolutely agree with all elements of the religious community's teachings. There are several reasons for involvement in a religious community like close, personal relationships or a general convenience of proximity. Yet, certain aspects could create conflicts for the devotee. For example, a committed Catholic might not agree that the priesthood should be restricted to celibate men but still attend Mass and identify as a Catholic. Or more extreme, while a religious community might exclude LGBTQ+ people, a member of that religious community might maintain close friendships with someone identifying as LGBTQ+ causing an internal conflict for that individual.

This section obviously removes some of the polish of sports and religions, which many people consider wholesome institutions. Devotees might simply remain in denial, as a coping mechanism, when a disconnect between their values and their favorite religious community or sporting institution emerges. In certain instances, individuals must learn to navigate their devotion to a sports team or a religious community while also adamantly disagreeing with specific elements occurring within those spaces. Luther and Davidson's work is filled with multiple examples including:

- Brain trauma and American football
- Doping/steroids/Human Growth Hormones
- Racist mascots
- Gender inequality
- Domestic violence by players

Correspondingly, a list of negative aspects of contemporary religions that could cause some devotees to cringe:

- Catholic paedophilia scandal
- Sexual abuse
- LGBTQ+ exclusion
- Inappropriate usage of finances
- Gender inequality
- Religious violence

These issues can obviously be devastating to those committed to a particular religion or sport. These conflicts can propel fans and devotees to reconsider their levels of commitment to these organizations. Should the individual continue their devotion or stop participating altogether? Can the devotee continue financially supporting an institution that excludes members based on sexuality when the individual's morals misalign with the organization? Is it time to find a new sport, team, or religious community? Should the devotee go into advocacy mode and attempt to reform the sport or religious community? What would advocacy look like in these situations?

As an exercise of reflection, take time to consider how sports or religions have disappointed the reader or a religious or sport devotee the reader knows. Take time to either journal about these thoughts or speak with another person about these issues. Discussing disappointment or harm done can be difficult. The reader should feel free to share in as much as they are comfortable and withhold any trauma too difficult to discuss. Some questions for consideration:

- Have you ever supported a team or player and been disappointed by something they did/said? What were the circumstances? What was your response?
- Has a religious leader or organization disappointed the reader? If so, in what ways? What was your response?
- Does the reader find that the negative elements outweigh the positive or the opposite? How does one go about weighing these issues?
- Do you know of a fan or devotee who has struggled with devotion to a team, player, or religion? If so, how?
- Have you seen changes for the good within a sports or religious organization? What did this look like? Did committed members advocate for the change?

SOCIAL JUSTICE, PROPHETS, AND ATHLETIC ACTIVISM

Historically, religious figures regularly voiced concerns over shared social affairs. As religious leaders focus attention on morals, ethics, and best life practices, these voices directed societies on how to improve their circumstances. Whether religious leaders instructed people in how to treat fellow citizens, conduct economics fairly, or what to do in situations like famine or war, religious leaders drew upon textual codes and historical precedents. This does not mean that religious leaders were always correct in their assessments or even neutral in their formulations. At some points in history, dissident religious voices have emerged to challenge the dominant religious authorities. Often called prophets, these individuals countered religious leaders with different solutions to the problems plaguing society. Hebrew or Jewish history is filled with such prophetic voices. As Christianity and Islam build from the Hebrew scriptures, they, too, incorporate prophets into their authority structures. Prophets typically operated outside of the traditional religious institutions seeking to connect with society in public places. Prophets also employed creative means to communicate their messages, which were often social critiques. For example, the prophet Isaiah transmitted his message while nude and Ezekiel devoured a scroll while lying on his side for over a year discussing the resurrection of dry bones. The responses to these prophetic messages seem to have varied widely, with some being offended, others showing some support, and some choosing to simply ignore the prophets. Significantly, the prophets and local religious leaders regularly engaged in critiques, admonishments, and reprimands of each other, and to political leaders of the time. This discourse between prophets and religious leaders captures the social conversations occurring in societies pertaining to how to respond to social problems.

Sociologist Max Weber (1922) devoted a significant amount of his studies to analyzing authority models in industrializing societies, including religious authority. Weber designed three different authority typologies (types or categories): legal/rational, traditional, and charismatic. The legal/traditional typology includes legal courts, police forces, and rules written in recorded documents. Religious leaders like priests and monks in accepted social institutions like churches and monasteries fall into Weber's traditional authority type with their power and influence in society relying on accepted cultural norms. Outside of any legal/rational or traditional form of authority, Weber contemplated historical religious figures like Jesus, Muhammad, and Siddhartha (the Buddha), who rejected the traditional religious authority but still attracted followers and devotees. Weber concluded these leaders fall into their own category of charismatic or prophetic figures, claiming they had a special gift of charisma. Outside of any legal/rational or traditional form of authority, Weber acknowledged the impact of these leaders while lacking the ability to specifically define from where their charisma originates.

As some societies secularize, the authority once granted to religious leaders and their institutions recedes. With religion's authority diminishing in some regions of the world, a gap is created for a shared resource for societies' members to consult during difficult times. If traditional authority types lose power, who fills the void created by this loss? One solution to this question that I theorized in a previous work (Shoemaker 2018) is that activist athletes are prophetic in their actions over the last century or so in the United States, often displacing religious leaders. Scholars examine "athlete activism" or "sports activism" because of the increasing relevance of athlete's voices in the contemporary world (Magrath 2022; Edwards 2017; Cooper et al. 2019; Moore 2017; Galily 2019). Behavioral scientist Yair Galily defines sports-based activism as "specific actions taken by athletes to alter and mitigate the hegemonic nature of structural arrangements, rules/policies/bylaws, and practices through sport organizations that serve to reinforce subordination, marginalization, and exploitation of certain groups" (2019, p. 1). As Galily properly notes, sports activism seeks to transform society for the better. One team of scholars details five types of athletic activism conducted specifically by black athletes including symbolic, scholarly, grassroots activism, sport-based activism, and economic activism (Cooper et al. 2019). Although varied, when certain athletes, often politically disenfranchised, attempt to disrupt practices, policies, or social norms regarding race, gender, sexuality, social class, etc., they are engaging in activism. Several well-known historical examples of athlete activists typically spring to mind like Muhammad Ali (boxer), Tommie Smith and John Carlos (Olympic runners), and Billie Jean King (tennis). Contemporary illustrations include WNBA Center

Brittney Griner and her team the Phoenix Mercury's partnering with Bring Our Families Home, an organization working to bring home innocent people detained overseas; England striker Marcus Rashford's advocacy campaign to ensure kids in England received free meals during the summer holidays; and USA soccer player Megan Rapinoe's determination to establish gender pay equality for female athletes. Using social media platforms and public events, the reach of sports activists leverages a global reach in order to apply pressure to local policies.

Connecting athlete activism with historical prophetic activity shows how sports activists facilitate a secular form of prophetic activity today. This can be seen clearly using Walter Brueggemann's (1978) framework of prophetic imagination applied to black, professional basketball activists. Biblical scholar Walter Brueggemann builds from Judeo-Christian historical examples while situating the prophet within the context of the contemporary United States. For Brueggemann, the prophet is always in dialectical tension with the dominant power structures of society, which he calls empire. Within this tension, the prophet articulates social critiques of imperial transgressions through making social injustices permeating society visible. Those in power are often blind or numb to these issues because these tend to happen in the margins of society. In other words, prophets work to disturb the empire's malaise. Following the critiques, which bring social sufferings to light, prophets energize listeners with an alternative vision for society that includes "promises of another time and situation toward which the community of faith may move" (p. 3). Brueggemann explains that prophetic energizing is necessary because simply critiquing the empire rarely brings about the necessary changes to make society more just, equitable, and fair. This new vision of society, when conveyed properly by the prophet, recruits a movement of followers willing to stand against the dominant systems regulating society – the legal/rational and traditional authorities to reference Weber's terminology.

Race divisions, racism, and systemic racism continue to plague American society as well as other communities across the globe. In 2014, the death of an unarmed, African-American male named Michael Brown by police officer Darren Wilson evoked a new movement of protests across the country. The circumstances surrounding Brown's death remain disputed, but Brown's lifeless body lay in the streets of Ferguson, Missouri, for over four hours before being removed and taken to the local morgue. This incident sparked civil unrest locally and nationally in the subsequent days, leading to national conversations about police brutality, the use of military equipment by local police, and police treatment of people of color. A new decentralized movement, later called Black Lives Matter (BLM), began organizing and protesting across the country. In the midst of these conversations and protests, professional basketball players (along with collegiate basketball players) began utilizing their platforms to articulate outrage and exasperation with police violence. WNBA players embraced the need to provide a jolt for society in 2017 when the Los Angeles Sparks team refused to be present on the court during the national anthem during the championship finals. The entire Sparks team remained in the locker room until the anthem was finished. This provocative move stood in direct opposition to the words of then-President Donald J. Trump who fumed against NFL football players, like Colin Kaepernick, kneeling during the national anthem. The Sparks team's absence during the national anthem counters the dominant performance of standing for the national anthem that signifies allegiance to the ideals, values, and practices of the nation-state. By not participating in the anthem, WNBA players signaled their discontent with policing violence against people of color. Additionally, WNBA players began media blackouts, refusing to speak after games, or wore warmup shirts listing the names of people of color killed by police. These actions created a symbolic and verbal critique of the dominant consciousness that police officers are inherently good and treat all individuals fairly and equally.

According to Brueggemann, more than a jolt is required for contemporary prophetic activity. Contemporary prophets should provide an energizing influence for others to pay attention to and stand against the dominant regime. One part of this invigoration came during the 2016 ESPY Awards ceremony, a ceremony conducted by ESPN to recognize numerous achievements of athletes, when Dwyane Wade, a guard for the Miami Heat, stated,

> Now as athletes it's on us to challenge each other to do even more than we already do in our communities. The conversation cannot stop, as our schedules get busy again. It won't always be convenient, it won't. It won't always be comfortable but it is necessary.
>
> (Chan 2016)

Wade stood on stage with other NBA All-Stars like LeBron James, Chris Paul, and Carmelo Anthony, and, together, they made a powerful plea against police brutality. Chris Paul proclaimed, "We stand here tonight accepting our roles in uniting communities" (Chan 2016). The moves of black professional athletes work toward building an alternative prophetic society. By using their platform to create opportunities for dialogue, the critique begins to take a dialogic shape that brings stakeholders together. Like the responses to historical figures, many people would simply reject the prophetic voices. Fox News anchor Laura Ingraham told LeBron James to "shut up and dribble" after he offered critiques of then-President Trump (Sullivan 2018). James responded by thanking Ingraham for opening up more opportunities for him to speak about social justice, keeping up the social critiques and energizing a movement promoting fairness and equality. After the ESPYs Carmelo Anthony helped organize a local meeting in Baltimore to discuss police violence in primarily black communities. Anthony stated, "We want to get community leaders, athletes, everybody having this conversation and talking on both sides hearing each other out. It's part of continuing what I started off" (Gomez 2016). Combined, the WNBA and NBA formed a strong alliance in bringing recognition to BLM-identified issues, advocated on behalf of community members, and organized local discussions around policing.

Brueggemann is clear that prophetic voices must completely understand the plight of the people for whom they speak. In his words, Brueggemann argues that prophets must be "children of the tradition" or "one who has taken [the tradition] seriously in the shaping of his or her field of perception and system of language, who is at home in that memory" (1978, p. 2). Black athletes are part of a rich African-American tradition historically offering counter frames to the American society, which presents itself as overwhelmingly fair, equitably, and just. This rich prophetic tradition is exemplified by Martin Luther King, Jr., but includes numerous black men, women, children, spirituals, liberation theologies, institutions, and organizations that draw upon African spirituality, Islam, and Christianity. Furthermore, these contemporary prophetic athletes build upon a wealth of historical examples of previous athletic activism from black athletes. In an American society with no singular religious leader or organization representing a majority of its members, religious voices do not carry the same impact as in previous generations. Instead, a few athletes, now idolized by millions of fans, embrace the role of prophetic voice championing causes. Although Brueggemann thought that the prophets would be connected with traditional forms of religion (like the Christian tradition), professional sporting organizations house the voices for critiquing, jolting, and providing hope for a different kind of society.

In this example, the dialogue occurring seems to circumvent traditional forms of religion. However, as Matthew Cressler notes, "Whereas the civil rights movement tended to be 'manned' by 'well-dressed, respectable clergymen,' the [Movement for Black Lives] is unapologetically feminist and queer" (2021, p. 17). Where black ministers and pastors led the moral charge against social injustices in the past, in the case of the Black Lives Matter (BLM) movement (the umbrella name for the protests against police brutality in America), black athletes, equipped with large-scale media platforms, articulated the public message along with local and national organizers. In the broader BLM movement, black ministers participated in local organizing and protests (Cressler 2021), but the public conversations point to a new authority, still prophetic in nature, in society: black athletes. In some situations, BLM organizers disagreed with religious leaders who attempted to assemble protests that looked more like the 1960s Civil Rights-era protests (Renaud and Wilder 2021). A planned protest in Chicago in 2015 over the death of Laquan McDonald created a "a case study of the real conversations that we need to have if we're going to have a movement that truly represents the wisdom of both generations," according to one BLM organizer (Renaud and Wilder 2021). Although some religious leaders and organizations played a role in the BLM movement, these organizations tended to be less central compared to previous civil rights movements.

As Forbes and Mahan note when it comes to dialogue between religion and popular culture, "religion wants to take part in the broader discussion" (2017, p. 19). The need to take part in the broader conversation is evidenced with how Pope Francis responded to the Black Lives Matter movement and the NBA's participation. Before moving into Pope Francis' response to the NBA and BLM, it is important to note that in 2016 the Vatican convened various leaders to discuss the connection between religions and sports. At that conference, Pope Francis quipped, "sport transcends the level of pure physicality and takes us into the arena of the spirit and even of mystery. And these moments are accompanied by great joy and satisfaction, which we all can share, even those not competing" (Brockhaus 2016). The pope's description of sport echoes earlier material that locates sports as religious activity or at least a mechanism through which humans can achieve a transcendence. With a foundation for understanding the cultural impact of sports related to religiosity, in the autumn of 2020, the Vatican requested an in-person meeting with NBA players to discuss their activism around race and policing issues. Specifically, one NBA representative stated that they discussed, "individual and collective efforts addressing social and economic injustice and inequality occurring in their communities" with the Vatican (Lowe 2020). This direct dialogue illustrates the power and influence of professional athletes and religious leaders in the world today. Being the religious leader of the largest religious community in the world, the Pope recognized the value in the prophetic work conducted by NBA players. Likewise, NBA players acknowledged the potential collaborative power of combining forces to tackle issues of inequality.

The emergence of black athletes engaging in sports activism in the United States coincides with people of color obtaining the legal right to participate in professional and collegiate sports. Systemic racism in the United States historically marginalized black athletes from competing, but also from using a sports platform to voice the concerns of black citizens. Disenfranchisement resulted in the black church being the central organizing location for civil rights protests. As more people of color secured college degrees and entry into professional sports, the black Christian church generationally has become less relevant (although the black church remains vital for people today). This situation provokes several critical questions regarding dialogue between religious leaders and sport activists today. First, is the dialogue about cooperation or competition? An answer to this must attempt to measure the influence of black religious leaders on the BLM movement. Is it the case that black religious leaders took a cooperative role to the BLM leadership in various cities or is it that black religious leaders attempted to exert their authority in these situations? Second, is there an unspoken displacement of authority occurring, which subsequently sidelines religious leaders? Do the prophetic athlete activists illustrate how religions, broadly speaking, are losing power and influence in some nations across the globe? Another consideration to this question might be whether black athlete activists are secular prophetic voices rather than religiously-inspired prophetic voices. Either way, athletes, both professional women's and men's basketball players, along with other athletes like Colin Kaepernick, constructed a new style of civil rights protest building from a rich prophetic tradition while integrating secular spaces as platforms.

SOCIAL JUSTICE, SOCIAL MEDIA, AND ATHLETES

With the emergence of social media, some athletes publicly share various types of information to devoted fans and trolls alike. From a consumer perspective, social media is a platform for athletes to cultivate their brand, supply information, and market products. In other words, social media fashions a commercial opportunity to advertise and self-promote. Athletes leverage these platforms hoping to acquire endorsement deals and increased salaries. Athletes also employ social media platforms like Twitter to discuss trades, wins/losses, and taunt other athletes. Yet, athlete's social media presentations and the athlete's branding are built upon both private and public aspects of the athlete's life. Sociologist Erving Goffman (1959) argues that individuals continually negotiate how to present themselves around others in different contexts to elicit positive responses. These presentations include both frontstage and backstage attempts to construct favorable reputations. Applied to athletes, "Scholars define athlete-based frontstage content as self-presentation depicting the athlete engaging in their chosen sport, whereas backstage content presents the athlete in personal settings" (Doyle et al. 2020, p. 3). For athletes, social media accounts project both frontstage and backstage information regarding the player's professional life as an athlete and their private life as a member of the society.

Lacking clear training in how to use social media accounts, some athletes run into trouble when they post inappropriate backstage or frontstage material on platforms like Facebook, X (formerly Twitter) or Instagram. Several case studies of basketball players demonstrate the missteps of some athletes in these matters. The NBA's Memphis Grizzlies player Ja Morant encountered fines and suspensions when he broadcasted himself with a gun, former Boston Celtics forward Paul Pierce posted racy images, which led to his termination as a sports analyst for ESPN, and Minnesota Timberwolves rising star Anthony Edwards posted a homophobic message and received a hefty fine from the NBA. Each of these situations occurred on Instagram with about a million followers for Pierce and Edwards and 10 million followers for Ja Morant. Unfortunately, these social media posts were probably seen by impressionable youth. Likewise, some professional athletes share negative events occurring during team practices or in the locker rooms like in-fighting or critiques of their teams. Professional athletes, like the rest of us, make mistakes, but because of their influence, their errors often face higher levels of scrutiny from fans, other players, and media pundits. For damage control purposes, these blundering athletes typically employ the same social media site to convey apologies and other messages to try to repair their reputations.

More positively, whether announcing the birth of a new baby or the death of a loved one, many athletes feel compelled or pressured to share aspects of their lives as a key component of their professional careers. These posts sometimes include athletes' sharing their views and opinions about all kinds of matters and also fall into the backstage presentations category. These matters might center on local, political debates that are quite inconsequential elsewhere or on national or global issues with broad-scale effects for millions of people. Since political issues are contested and heavily debated, these posts carry with them a level of risk for the athlete's image. If a fan's perspective on a specific issue disagrees with an athlete's perspective on the same issue, this could lead to some fans disavowing their devotion to the athlete, which can also result in financial losses. On the flip side, if fans overwhelmingly approve of the athlete's stance on a topic, there could be financial as well as social gains for the athlete. As it pertains to social justice stances, athletes must consider how their proclamations might affect their branding. For all-star athletes with high levels of celebrity status, there might be losses to consider, but varying degrees of impact overall to their branding.

Whether positive or negative, the usage of social media creates an interactive dialogue between athletes and fans. In fact, most social media platforms are built to facilitate discussion. NBA player Jason Collins' story provides a case study illustrating the ways in which sports dialogue occurs and how religion engages with these conversations. In 2013, Collins announced in a *Sports Illustrated* article that he was gay. Although many WNBA players openly discussed their sexuality, before this announcement, no active male NBA player had admitted openly to being homosexual. Collins received several positive responses on Twitter and traditional media with a "celebratory and congratulatory tone, emphasizing Collins' coming out as a significant 'first,' a 'watershed moment' for gay rights" (Billings et al. 2015, p. 153). In addition to the general support from celebrities and other athletes, one media analysis discovered that religion was a prevailing theme in the initial days following Collins' announcement. Some of these tweets questioned or critiqued the idea that Collins could identify as both gay and Christian since some Christians interpret their religious text as condemning homosexuality. For example, "ESPN basketball analyst Chris Broussard stated that he did not believe that Collins could 'live an openly homosexual lifestyle' and be a Christian, but thought that Collins 'displayed bravery with his announcement'" (as quoted in Billings et al. 2015, p. 153). Collins admitted that he grappled with how being Christian and gay correlated. A decade after coming out publicly, he said this about religion:

> Religion should not be a cause for division, to justify any kind of inequality or to not be able to accept someone for who they are…It's about bringing people together. That's what I think religion should be about. It's unfortunate when people aren't that way and try to use religion as a way to divide.
>
> (Sayles 2023)

Collins' perspective on religion as a unifying force belies the fact that some religious people questioned his sexuality and religiosity's compatibility.

The Jason Collins story highlights the need to conduct more intersectional analyses when examining particular religions and sports. Intersectional research considers how multiple forms of identity, like race and gender, play a role in specific scenarios. An intersectional analysis could interrogate why Collins and other male athletes tend to be less accepted by some for being gay in comparison to female athletes. For example, Brittney Griner, Phoenix Mercury star in the WNBA, came out as gay before Collins with less push back. Lori Dann and Tracy Everbach argue, "Women athletes have long been stereotyped as lesbians, whereas male athletes are portrayed as the pinnacle of heterosexual masculinity" (2016, p. 170). Integrating gender into the conversation allows us to better understand that people accept Griner's announcement as an "of course" while they push back against Collins' sexuality. Adding to the scenario, Collins is an African-American male athlete, and black male athletes are often stereotyped as hypermasculine. Collins' sexuality challenges held stereotypes about black, male athletes. A decade after coming out as gay, Collins admits the complexity still surrounding sexuality, race, and athletes today:

> It's a constant struggle and fight for equality. You can celebrate marriage equality but know the next day you've got to fight just to keep it or keep on advancing. There are some very conservative people out there who want to walk things back in time, and we cannot let that happen.
>
> (Sayles 2023)

Individuals are multidimensional with myriad identities. Being a pro athlete and religious only tells part of someone's story.

Through considering a player's sexuality, race, gender, and religious identity more holistically, we realize that a conglomeration of individual identities inform the decisions and actions people make. The examinations should include race, gender, and religion along with one's sporting affiliation. Thus, sports and religions are only part of the complicated equation. When a player posts on Instagram or X they often post frontstage material about their sporting life, relegating backstage information to a more private space. However, backstage information often moves centerstage when athletes decide to push against accepting social norms or challenge social expectations. This evokes interactive conversations about the athletes, but, more generally, about human experience. A black, male professional basketball player with a religious affiliation announcing his homosexuality publicly might encourage some to jump into broader conversations about equality, diversity, and inclusion and how some are resistant to these ideas.

BOX 5.2 SOCIAL MEDIA AND SOCIAL JUSTICE

Although most social media platforms grant individuals the option to post publicly or privately, a large number of athletes continue to use social media platforms in a public manner. This creates a wealth of data for social scientists, communication scholars, and those interested in the content of these postings. As an exercise, take time to compare and contrast social media posts by athletes. These might include very famous athletes or those who are less well-known. What does the social media content look like for these athletes? Who is active? Who is not? Do the posts focus on the sport, game, team, or season primarily? In other words, does the athlete compartmentalize their athletic life from their personal life and post frontstage content? Or does the athlete post backstage content indicating political, religious, or social preferences and positions? What does this material look like? Are there trends in when and what gets posted on specific days or weeks? What are the athletes reacting to?

Now take a moment to evaluate the identity information of the athletes. Are there differences in what athletes post based on gender? What type of conclusions can be drawn from comparing and contrasting male and female athletes' social media accounts? What does this reveal about the society in which they live? Does race seem to factor in creating differences between the athletes' posts? If so, how? Are there similarities between athletes of specific sports (i.e. do baseball players tend to share similar content)? Does integrating an intersectional lens help us better understand society and individual perceptions as it relates to this content? For example, take into consideration both race and gender and see if conclusions can be drawn from the data. Do white, female professional athletes' social media consist of generally different material than their black, female colleagues? Or, for instance, do white, female professional athletes' social media posts look different than black, male professional athletes?

To take this exercise one step further, now review the responses to the posts. Are female athletes targeted with oversexualized or misogynistic replies? What kinds of replies are there to posts from minoritized professional athletes? Do racial slurs show up in this investigation? If so, when and where? What does this reveal about society? Do transexual athletes face more or less discrimination than cisgendered athletes? Again, how does applying an intersectional analysis (e.g. racially minoritized and female) show different levels of negative responses to posts?

When conducting research like this, spreadsheets or hand-made charts aid in being able to compare collected data. Maybe create a chart or spreadsheet to show data differences highlighting important aspects of the data. Take time to discuss this material with others who are conducting similar analyses.

CHAPTER SYNOPSIS

Beyond personal expression, sports and religions occupy a space in society for discussing social issues. Due to societies imbuing religious leaders and athletes with social influence, their opinions and perspectives carry a significant clout, whether this be a religious leader criticizing a social or legal policy or an athlete doing the same. In some societies today, religious leaders maintain a central authority. These religious leaders draw upon historical precedents and sacred texts to propose solutions and diagnoses of social ills.

In other societies, the diminishing authority of religious leaders and organizations creates a void where other voices, like professional athletes, can fill the vacancy of authority. In this chapter, we examined the role of professional athletes in offering social critiques specifically on issues of race. These athletes build upon their social status to speak out on issues plaguing minoritized communities of color in the United States. Like the prophets of old, athletes today take a stand on public platforms (i.e. social media) to detail the transgression of the society and propose an alternative way of being. These prophets, as I have called them, build upon the previous athletic athleticism of black athletes and the prophetic traditions of the black church in the United States. This results in a religio-secular form of prophetic activity.

Similarly, in a few instances, direct dialogues between professional athletes and religious leaders form. The case of Pope Francis discussing race relations with NBA athletes demonstrates a direct attempt to work together to ameliorate race issues. This brings an increased awareness to these issues through capitalizing on the influence and power of both athletes and religious leadership. As issues require collective organizing and input to remedy, bringing together religious and sporting institutional voices creates a more powerful prestige able to leverage their clout to inspire people to consider their role in solving social problems.

This chapter also reminds us that humans carry various identities that inform their activities and perspectives. Adopting an intersectional approach to examining case studies provides a more holistic analysis. A combination of individual and collective sexual, racial, ethnic, and religious identities influence decision making and positions. To ignore some identities over others doesn't tell the entire story; thus, limiting studies to only religious and sporting identities reduces the validity of the overall results to studies. Intersectional approaches produce a complex picture of human practices and responses to certain scenarios. Sometimes these identities conflict or need negotiating. When a sports fan encounters a troublesome scenario, like when a favorite athlete makes an inappropriate racial statement, they must decide how to navigate their fan devotion and their moral compass. Social media advances these conversations and forms a significant amount of data for analysis.

RECOMMENDED READING

This chapter tackles several important topics related to society and religions' and sports' role in those matters. The increase in athlete or sports activism over the last decade yields an increase in scholarly accounts of these activities. The following books supply past and contemporary resources of a handful of books explicating athlete and sports activism. Harry Edwards' (2017, 50th anniversary edition) *The Revolt of the Black Athlete* and William Rhoden's (2006) *Forty Million Dollar Slaves* remain essential reading for understanding how race impacts the lives of black athletes in the United States. In addition to these works, several edited volumes examine multiple angles and sports across the globe. *No Slam Dunk: Gender, Sport and the Unevenness of Social Change* (2018), edited by Cheryl Cooky and Michael Messner, investigates gender inequalities within sports today. Editor Mia Long Anderson's (2023) volume, *Social Justice and the Modern Athlete: Exploring the Role of Athlete Activism in Social Change* composes a strong investigation of several social issues with athlete involvement. Finally, Rory Magrath's (2022) *Athlete Activism: Contemporary Perspectives* provides some international case studies as well as the role of disabilities in athlete activism.

RELIGIONS AND SPORTS IN COMPETITION

The previous chapters explore relationships between religions and sports. These relationships indicate various ways of situating the overlaps, intersections, and interfacing of religious individuals, communities, and institutions vis-a-vis athletes, fans, coaches, and institutions. Understanding religions and sports as categories, concepts, and spaces forms analyses where we can illustrate where they intersect. For instance, some religious communities adopt different types of sports for their usage in disciplining members or advancing their agendas. Likewise, athletes and coaches sometimes bring their religiosity or faith into sporting arenas. There are debates about whether sports and religions should intermingle as much as they do. Furthermore, our review thus far, following Forbes and Mahan's frames, informs us of how religions and sports dialogue and the possibility of sports functioning similarly to religious practices. In the case of the former, some religious leaders perceive discussing specific issues with athletes as advantageous. Creating a public sphere of dialogue with athletes and religious leaders generates ideas, positions, and sometimes partnerships to tackle shared and recognized social ills. Due to athletes maintaining such a prominent role in societies, they can offer influential social critiques. Although not all agree, sports mirror some religious aspects for some individuals who potentially wouldn't recognize their practices and fan commitments as religious. As religions and sports are human ventures, they can functionally meet human needs, and these needs and fulfillment of the needs mimic the other. These topics will obviously be debated further.

DOI: 10.4324/9781003362630-6

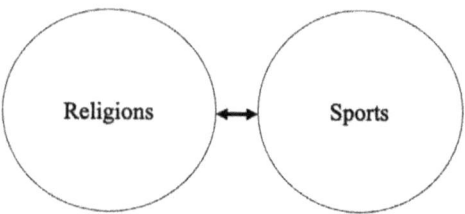

Figure 6.1

This chapter reviews another angle, complementing Forbes and Mahan, to approach the topic of sports and religions. Although Forbes and Mahan propose four angles for examining religion and popular culture, the study of religions and sports warrants at least one additional angle: the competition between religions and sports. As competition constitutes a key aspect of most sports and games, it provides an angle from which to consider both sports and religions and their relationship (Figure 6.1). This angle in the relationship of sports and religions considers individuals as consumers first with numerous options and choices. Although it might be difficult initially to understand religions as markedly competitive, we will see that in a cultural marketplace, religious organizations and institutions contend for members, time commitments, and financial investments much in the same way that sports do. Once we place religions and sports within a cultural marketplace, we can better envision how sports and religions compete for individual commitments. In this section, I draw on my research projects, thinking about how sports and religions might compete. These examples demonstrate how qualitative and quantitative studies can provide insight, not a full assessment, of specific phenomena related to sports and religions. First, let's examine the cultural marketplace.

CULTURAL MARKETPLACE

As members of societies, most humans balance various domains of life. Philosopher Robert Cummins (1996) posits several discrete domains of life – health, productivity, material wellbeing, intimacy, safety, emotional wellbeing, and community – which need proper ordering to develop a satisfied life. A key aspect of being able to order life includes the accessibility of resources. For maintaining or improving quality of life, people look to various cultural sources and numerous options exist today in the marketplace of products and resources. With communication and transportation, the marketplace supplies resources from across the globe. For example, clothing, medicines, and food products are exported across national borders, and the market is responsive to human activity and issues like war and conflicts. With online access to products and globalization, consumers truly are inundated with product placement daily. Cultural ideas and resources also exist within the marketplace. Popular bands and artists create musical products that either resonate with fans or don't. Political ideologies permeate online forums for better or worse. The global cultural marketplace, grounded in Internet, communication, and shipping technologies, provides opportunities for numerous innovators to form new supplies meeting market demands for individual and collective wellbeing.

The supply and demand relationship results in both positives and negatives for individual consumers. The market of competing products creates conditions where suppliers must manufacture, advertise, and convince consumers that their products are essential and of the best quality. The task of the supplier then is to evaluate needs and material desires and offer resources to fulfill those needs. Consumers in the marketplace maintain the ongoing and difficult tasks of deciding which products to purchase and utilize for their particular needs and wants. With the globalized market, consumers might find themselves inundated with marketing and product options. Sociologist Barry Schwartz (2004) discusses the stress and responsibilities associated with making consumer choices from the hundreds of options available in his book *The Paradox of Choice*. In his work, Schwartz suggests that the sheer number of available options in the cultural marketplace overwhelms some consumers, actually creating emotional and mental stress. Whether a plethora of positive or negative options is necessarily good is left to the reader, but what Schwartz's study indicates is how problematic hundreds of choices for most consumers today can be. In sum, as individuals attempt to balance various domains of life, there exists an infinite supply of resources promoted as improvements for daily life.

Zooming out broadly on religions and sports, we can map them within the cultural marketplace of ideas and resources. As a remedy for life's monotony, for example, some might seek sports to counter the more boring aspects of life. Sports can supply excitement and collective energy in order to relieve boredom. Others might seek out a religious leader or text as a means of finding a similar kind of fulfillment against life's more banal conditions. Moreover, consumers simply might consume the entertainment or leisure value of sports and religions. Religious organizations and sporting options compete with other forms of entertainment and leisure options available to consumers. Does an individual want to spend their time socializing at a mall or joining a soccer league? Does a consumer opt to attend a religious service weekly or invest their time in an online forum discussing hobbies or collectibles like antique cars? When making this decision, consumers prioritize their values and wants while weighing financial costs or time commitments. Additionally, some consumers might conduct a cost/benefit analysis: if I participate in a hockey league, what will it cost me in potential injuries or health benefits compared to participating in a dance class considering similar positive or negative outcomes? It is up to consumers to navigate and negotiate the marketplace of options.

Particular sports also exist in direct competition with other sports as well. This inner competition might seem obvious on a professional level. Sporting institutions compete for fans and product sales. How does a state's or nation's team capture the majority of citizens' fandom commitments? What if the state or nation sponsors teams in multiple sports? Will a hockey team in a city or state compete with a soccer team with an overlapping calendar and schedule? These teams might incentivize the sporting events with promotions or a halftime performance to secure a fan's attention. Direct competition also occurs at the amateur level for people playing recreational sports and other games. Whether an individual takes up volleyball, basketball, or hockey will be determined by numerous factors including interests, athletic abilities, the individual's health considerations, etc. There might be some pressures from family and local community members for some individuals to take up or continue to play certain sports. For instance, a town committed to soccer might heavily invest in training camps to develop future athletes for the team. There is a significant variety of sporting options depending on specific regions and places around the globe. Still, few people have the time, finances, or ability to play all sports or attend all religious gatherings.

Religious communities and institutions operate similarly. Rodney Stark and William Bainbridge (1996) propose that a marketplace of religious options exists wherein religious organizations and communities operate as sellers of religious goods in a market, and religiously-inclined individuals must make rational choice decisions for these goods. These goods could include otherworldly promises, life advice, or affirmation of one's values and goals. An individual might find that their beliefs and values align with a specific religious institution; however, they may very well determine there are numerous religious institutions with similar values and beliefs available to them, so something like musical differences determines how a selection could be made. Like shopping for a daycare for a child, there are numerous factors for religious consumers to consider when selecting their religious options: reputation, affordability, values alignment, etc. These selections might even be temporary. A religious consumer might find that the religious offerings (products) of an institution meet their needs for a duration of time in their life but that those needs change, prompting a re-evaluation of their religious choices. Moreover, with the availability of online religious options, like live-streamed religious services, choices are not limited by geographical location. Obviously, there are global examples wherein individuals legally maintain little religious options and freedom, but, overall, within the cultural marketplace, religious consumers can take advantage of multiple offerings and products.

As religions and sports directly compete within their category (i.e., religious community X competes with religious community Y), they also indirectly compete in a more expansive marketplace. Thus, sports compete with religions which compete with holiday planning which compete with educational attainment. This list could be greatly expanded. Individuals must decide where to invest their time, energy, and finances in an ever-competitive global economy. Professional marketers and business entrepreneurs know this and work to spotlight their products with online advertising, billboards, mailings, etc. Once an individual's initial attention is steered toward the product, then the supplier must work to further develop a commitment to the product and to maintain that commitment. Sports and religious marketing teams devote themselves to this work. Individuals operate as consumers determining their commitments to specific institutions or products. Within this decision making, religions and sports are two products available to them in the marketplace. In the following, we take a closer look at the spiritual marketplace and then examine two research examples that detail how the marketplace helps us understand the competition between religions and sports.

> ### BOX 6.1 THE SPIRITUAL MARKETPLACE
>
> In capitalist societies, there is a wide variety of choices available to individuals and groups. Think about the variety of music genres or types of movies available. An individual can choose a specific genre and live within the genre. For instance, a person might choose to *only* listen to hip-hop music. However, individuals can also take advantage of the diversity of available options and listen to hip-hop, pop music, and rock 'n' roll music. There is an artistic marketplace available to people who can access music. Similarly, a spiritual marketplace exists within some countries (Roof 1999). As spirituality maintains a level of unregulated, free-market enterprise, innovative spiritual entrepreneurs offer an array of spiritual products and options. The same is true of religion. Think about the exceptional assortment of types of religions and spiritual organizations today. Should an individual be dissatisfied with one aspect of one religious community, they can choose to invest their time and energy in another. Spiritual products operate similarly. If a consumer of spiritual oils finds that the product no longer satisfies their expectations, they can shop around the spiritual marketplace for a replacement product. Danièle Hervieu-Leger (2000) refers to this phenomenon as spiritual shopping. Spiritual shopping allows consumers to freely determine what, where, when, and how they form a subjective form of religiosity or spirituality.
>
> Spirituality is a complicated and (re)emerging term used in both scholarship and everyday parlance. Spiritual or spirituality stands

close to religion either in an almost indistinguishable manner or in contradiction. Forming a definition of spirituality can certainly be a difficult task. One group of scholars found "spirituality is increasingly characterized as 'personal and subjective'" (Zinnbauer et al. 1997). This definition is compared to religion, where religion is often understood as collective and social. Others try to work out different types of spirituality. These include a spectrum of commitments like the religiously devout, religious seekers, seekers of well-being, and nonreligious persons (Koenig 2008). Notice that in these typologies religious people can be spiritual just as the nonreligious might identify as spiritual. Furthermore, spirituality can denote intentional modes of individual discovery since some consumers are skeptical of religious and political institutions. Philip Sheldrake posits, "spirituality is frequently understood to involve a quest for meaning (including the purpose of life) as a response to the decline of traditional religious or social authorities" (2012, p. 5). Thus, as religion declines in more developed countries, spirituality emerges as an individual search to explore one's subjectivity.

At an organizational or institutional level, spiritual and religious communities and individuals are not immune from the influences of capitalism and corporatization. Although some communities might seek to ignore or take an agnostic posture toward the cultural marketplace, their members (or consumers) are still influenced by the market in their daily lives. Some religious organizations position themselves as opposed to much of the cultural marketplace offerings. They perceive the options in the cultural marketplace as superfluous or corruptive. Some take the opposite approach and embrace forms of popular culture within their communities as a means of religious or spiritual instruction. Either way, ignoring the competitive products available to individuals is increasingly difficult.

Ultimately, examining spiritual products available in the marketplace gives a small glimpse into how forces, like market-driven capitalism, propel a considerable amount of what occurs in spirituality and religions. What are the spiritual resources available to consumers? This is a tremendously broad question because of the sheer number of offerings available in the marketplace. As an exercise, take some time to visit websites (e.g., Goop.com) or a local store to get a better grasp of the spiritual products advertised and available for individual or group usage. Take some notes while

> paying attention to what the products are, what the products are purported to do for consumers, and the marketing language used to sell the products. What are the typical products like? A deeper analysis of these products should create further questions: Who purchases these products? Who makes the products? How successful are the manufacturers? Where are the products sold? What do you think catches the consumer's attention more compared to similar products of a spiritual nature? Do these products emphasize a "spiritual experience" (experiential value) or does the product have more of a concrete, functional value? Which companies and stores offer the supplies for a religious or spiritual demand? Who are the demographics of the average consumer?

SKATEBOARDING IN A SPIRITUAL MARKETPLACE

Skateboarding can be defined as a sport, mode of transportation, recreational activity, or an art form. The skateboard was introduced as a toy in the late 1940s, but over the decades, skateboarding became a cultural phenomenon with a distinctive associated lifestyle, films, video games, and ethos (Borden 2019). As skateboarding developed, the skateboard deck changed as speed and tricks emerged. As skateboarding's popularity increased, new types of rubber-soled shoes and attire flourished in skating. Skateboarders credited with developing modern skateboarding mimicked surfing in urban, often concrete spaces where ocean waves were not available or were inaccessible. This involved skating in storm drains, drained backyard pools, and schoolyards, often illegally. Contest skating coexisted with skateboarding since the 1960s; however, it began as a very different type of skateboarding that involved fancy footwork and spins. These elements still exist in modern skateboarding, but today's skateboarding involves more physical obstacles like ramps, handrails, and curbs. Contest skating gained popularity in the 1980s, with skaters like Tony Hawk legitimizing skateboarding as a form of play and profession. This eventually evolved into financial profitability, marketability, and exposure with the emergence of the X-Games, Street League, and, recently, the 2020 Olympics.

An abbreviated history of skateboarding reveals the growing popularity commercially and in the amateur field but doesn't address the question: what are skateboarders' perceptions of skating? Paul O'Connor's (2017) research situates skateboarding as a spiritual practice with sacred sites, much like other sporting arenas deemed holy by fans and athletes. He argues, "skateboarding is not unlike other sports in the sense of history surrounding placemaking" (p. 1664). Like the religious aspect of demarcating a specific site as sacred due to a recognized historical event, skateboarders also demarcate particular sites as sacred because of events, like the first time a trick was landed. Furthermore, O'Connor's (2019) more exhaustive work situates skateboarding as functionally religious. In his *Skateboarding and Religion*, O'Connor contends religion in skateboarding is a performative and meditative act as a "DIY (Do It Yourself) religion" (O'Connor 2019). This allows skateboarders the opportunity to construct a religiosity as they see fit. Skateboarding creates experiences of transcendence and cultivates *communitas* (community), where the audience taps into shared experiences of the highs and lows of skating. O'Connor's research provides details of the collective experience of skateboarding.

To build upon O'Connor's work, a colleague and I (Shoemaker and Bernal 2024) decided to interview skateboarders in the Phoenix, Arizona, area to ascertain how they describe skating. Our specific research inquiry devoted attention to whether skateboarders would describe skateboarding as a religious or spiritual exercise. As a method of research, we adopted a qualitative approach. Our target goal included trying to interview at least 30 skaters at three primary skateparks around the greater Phoenix area. We chose Phoenix out of convenience but also because Phoenix's hot and arid weather lends itself to skateboarding. Our qualitative approach would allow us to speak directly with skateboarders and ask them why they skated. Strategically, we decided not to ask skaters directly if they thought skating was analogous to a religious or spiritual activity. Instead, we asked more indirect, general questions like "What is skateboarding to you?" and "How would you describe skating?" Within the data we collected from interviewing over 30 skateboarders, we discovered that a majority of our interviewees found the practice of skateboarding as spiritual. While only a few actually utilized the term spiritual directly, a majority used descriptors closely associated with spiritual or religious practices. The following selected quotes are illustrative of the interviews:

> I love skating alone sometimes. *It can be like meditating.* Just you in your head thinking about the tricks you want to do and nothing else.

> Through skateboarding, I've almost died. I've rolled my ankles more times than I can count. I've destroyed my hips and knees (some mornings I can barely walk). I've hit my face on the ground, sprained both of my wrists, been covered in road rash and bruises, and I'd do it all over again without even thinking about it! *Skateboarding is my spirituality.* It has gotten me through tough times, allowed me to make friends around the world, taught me patience & perseverance, and given me a different perspective of the environment around me. I will do it until I can't walk at all.

> Infinity and it represents openness. [It's] a lifestyle for inventor minds. Skateboarding is falling down and getting back up. Inventing. Playing for the sake of playing. Toying around. That is why I do it and what I feel from my participation is *similar to meditation,* like a lulled-out, relaxed state, the very act of riding the board changes the way you move through life.

Although the data are not representative of all skateboarders everywhere, most of our interviewees described their skateboarding activities as meditative, spiritual, or used similar language.

As we dug further into the data, we wanted to know exactly what it was about skateboarding that resonated as spiritual. After our data analysis, we realized how the movement of the skateboarder's body, the urban environment of concrete sidewalks, metal railings, and scuffed curbs, and the risk-taking involved in attempting skateboarding tricks formed a spiritual exercise. These three elements combined to create an intense experience for skaters. Contorting the human body while riding a skate deck while manipulating an urban environment places the individual skater in a degree of danger, and skaters tend not to shy away from the risks. As one of the interviewed skaters explained, "[Falling is] the biggest thing in skateboarding. We fall way more than we land shit. You got to pay your dues to get good. Break a bone, man!" The risk factors involved in skating emerged in every interview. Skaters embraced risks rather than attempted to completely avoid them:

> You don't always wanna [sic] land stuff, you know? And that's [how] you know you're alive because you almost died kind of thing.

> If they take slam after slam then land a crazy trick it's amazing! It just shows you how hard it is and how much passion these guys have.

In fact, falling off the board serves as a rite of passage for serious skaters. The failure to accomplish the trick lays a foundation by which the successful landing is judged. Skaters must put in the hard work and bodily punishment if they are to be considered members of the skating community. The scars and stories of failure form social bonds and communal identities around these shared experiences. The following two excerpts illustrate this point:

> Falling is easily half the battle, if not more. That's the rite of passage to being a 'skateboarder.' It's not your friend. It hardly likes you. And it will put you in your place real quick.

> Falling down is a force in skateboarding that none can escape. It's how you get back up and cope with how falling makes you feel. Falling creates fear. Overcoming fear is a catalyst for success.

The shared experiences around failure and success offer an emotional outlet to distress from life's anxieties. One skateboarding interviewee offered his perspective: "Skateboarding helps get your mind off of things you may not want to think about. This could be stressors, family troubles, or things going on in your friends' lives." Skateboarding's inclusion and recognition of emotional release correspond to one medical study on spirituality finding that certain physical exercises resulted in the subsiding of anger toward one's self and provided "a doorway...to release their anger and welcome love of self" (Greenwood and Delgado 2011, p. 951). In a world often over-regulated (think about school and work schedules), skateboarding permits an opportunity to make one's own rules, innovate, and take chances that might appear irrational to outside observers.

Skateboarding is a release or escape, recurring words in our interviews, from the expectations placed on individuals in the contemporary world.

Combined with the risk taking and the stress relief, skateboarding also creates opportunities for skaters to manipulate urban environments in creative ways. Many spiritual practices locate opportunities for spiritual training within natural environments. Think of the numerous forests, rivers, and outdoor landscapes associated with spiritual retreats. Skaters adapt to their urban environments of concrete, metal railings, and stairs in order to discover artistic ways that they can become one with that environment. One skater explained: "I don't see skateboarding as a sport but a way to navigate and manipulate an urban environment in ways you see fit." Another echoed these sentiments and explained the feelings involved with skating: "Rolling around the park while listening to music allows me to get into a creative and surf-like flow that I may super focus in on or zone out during." These responses emphasize the role of the environment in the spirituality of skateboarding. Finding sidewalks, parking lots, and streets more accessible, skateboarders transform the mundane to the sacred. In sum, these skaters ascribe spiritual meaning to their skateboarding activities.

The findings shouldn't have been surprising since many spiritual and religious practices utilize the environment and the physical body to offer an element of risk for devotees. Some meditation practices push individuals to extend the limits of their breathing. Additionally, people tend to find spiritual resonances when hiking outdoors, much like our skateboarding interviewees recognized something special about city environments. Although using different elements in different spaces, skateboarding is a spiritual practice in the contemporary world for the study's skateboarders. This obviously doesn't mean that skating is spiritual for all skaters; however, we wouldn't imagine that meditation is spiritual for all meditators. Likewise, many people look to religious and spiritual gatherings as a release from society's expectations. There are numerous reasons people employ and participate in specific practices.

Importantly, skateboarding as a spiritual practice situates skateboarding in a spiritual marketplace of options for consumers. Some spiritual practitioners might choose yoga or Reiki, while others might opt for skateboarding, kung fu, or running ultramarathons. It is easy to imagine the thousands of options an individual could select for spiritual activity. Individuals are not limited to one option either. Some might decide to practice more than one of these options. It is easy to imagine that a person could run marathons, practice yoga, and meditate, creating an individual slate of spiritual practices. This reflects the notion of a spiritual buffet of options where individuals choose what works for them at that moment of life. In this way sports and spiritual practices are both competitive and complementary. Yet, we can also imagine that some skateboarders might reject more traditional forms of religiosity in order to commit more fully to skating. After all, consumers simply cannot employ all products available; there are too many options. Religions, spiritual practices, and sporting options often compete for consumers' attention and investment.

Thanks to this skateboarding research project, we can understand how some forms of sports and play are considered, from an individual perspective, spiritual or religious. This does not mean that all people would equate sports with religiosity or spirituality. Instead, consumers make individual choices regarding what supplies are available and how to categorize those options. It is up to the consumer to determine how to use the products; therefore, consumers will perceive the products differently. Using a cultural marketplace lens reveals the multifaceted aspects of life lived in capitalist societies. A critique and limitation of a project like the qualitative research interviewing skateboarders revolves around to what extent the data are generalizable. Notice in the discussion that I made sure to indicate that the perspectives of a small sample of skateboarders in the greater Phoenix area might not correspond to other skaters in Phoenix or elsewhere. Certainly, other skaters in different cultural and national locations, as well as other states in the United States, might maintain differing perspectives. I like to imagine that qualitative projects are a small part of a much larger puzzle. Other researchers can take this project and build upon it by adding in their data. Slowly the broader puzzle image of skateboarding and spirituality develops.

BOX 6.2 QUALITATIVE INTERVIEWING EXERCISE

The skateboarding research project conducted by my research team, and referenced in the preceding section, is a qualitative research project. As noted early in the first chapter, qualitative research is a key aspect of studying cultural phenomena and religious studies. Qualitative projects typically include interviews (like talking with skateboarders) and observational data (watching and taking notes about what people do and how they do it). These studies supply a granular portrait of daily life for people across the globe. For example, what we learned about skateboarding gives insight into how skateboarders think about skateboarding beyond skating brands, types of tricks performed, or where one skateboards. Qualitative research supplies a "grounded approach," where data reveals information about what is occurring on the ground.

To construct a qualitative project involves more than merely taking to the streets and interviewing people. Instead, there are several steps involved in creating a qualitative research study. First, universities and colleges require human subject review (or institutional review board approval) for any study involving human subjects. As some researchers in the past have conducted unethical studies on humans, committees at universities decide the ethical nature of studies. Check with university protocols if qualitative interviews are being conducted in a classroom setting.

Before conducting any interviews, establish a research inquiry or problem. As a reminder, a research problem or inquiry is the specific issue that you are trying to resolve or explore within a research project. The primary research question guides the research project, narrows down the scope of the project, and helps the researcher stay focused. My research inquiry for the preceding project was simply "How do skateboarders describe skating and what are the important elements of skating?" Feel free to revisit Chapter 1 to review how to create a research inquiry.

Once the research question is established, the researcher needs to consider what population sample can best help address the inquiry. There are numerous approaches to deciding the sample population. For some questions, the research might target a group of religious elites or professionals. This could include rabbis, imams, ministers, or other leaders who are trained to lead and guide those under their direction. This would be a fairly large sample pool. Or the research could focus very specifically on a sample population, for example, female collegiate athletes playing lacrosse. This would significantly narrow the number of potential interviewees for the project, potentially creating difficulties in obtaining volunteers. Ultimately, the researcher must consider access to the sample population weighed with the research project's purpose.

After the research inquiry and the population is determined, the next step will be designing an interview guide. The interview guide is a series of questions to be addressed during the interview. This guide helps the researcher stay focused on the research inquiry and establishes uniformity. These questions might include demographic questions like the age and gender identity of the interviewee, as well as specific questions like "why do you play sport X" or prompts like "tell me about your religious journey." The researcher typically isn't restricted to only asking questions listed on the guide; instead, should an interviewee offer an interesting response, the researcher could ask follow-up questions. However, by using a uniform set of questions, the researcher will be better prepared to compare the data.

The researcher might look for common themes or outlying data when analyzing the data. Were similar stories, perspectives, or understandings shared with the researcher, forming an emerging theme? What was expected and unexpected? Did the responses surprise the researcher? If so, consider what the assumptions driving the research were. During the analysis processes, there are ways to code the data to provide anonymity to the interviewee and create a schematic for data analysis. There is also software available to assist with the analysis. Some of these are free and/or available to some university students.

This is only an introduction to conducting qualitative research. The processes can include in-depth software analysis, comparative samples, or interview guides. Scholars trained in the social sciences and anthropology could be consulted for more information regarding qualitative projects. One way to learn about conducting qualitative research is to construct a research problem and project using the information supplied here. Regarding religions and sports, what will be the question to be addressed? What will be the interview questions, and who will be interviewed? What is expected from the data?

SPORTS, RELIGIONS, AND TIME COMMITMENTS

One often frustrating aspect of human existence in the contemporary world is living with the reality of time restraints. The limitation on time emerges within our work, family, and leisure time. People wish for more time to finish a project at work or admit, simply, that time just ran out. "There's only so much time in a day" is an excuse offered for not being able to complete specific tasks. Some people commit too much time to work and, instead, would rather use their time with family. The pressures of work production can compel individuals to consider how to make the time for other aspects of life. This could include taking children to special events or vacations. Parents proclaim about their children: "they grow up so quickly." This references a perceived idea that time moves too fast. Our limitations of time can result in stress, poor sleeping habits, and intense decision making.

Within a cultural marketplace, humans must decide where to spend their time. (Think about how capitalism influences our culture – we *spend* our time.) How do people prioritize their time commitments with the ever-present attempt not to waste the time we have? There are numerous factors to take into consideration. Let's consider the parental decision to devote time to religious commitments. Family responsibilities could either prompt parents or guardians to commit their family to a religious community or not for the sake of their children. The parents' personal experience often influences this decision. External factors might influence the decision making processes. Social pressures from grandparents, invitations from those within their social network, or the compulsion to train their kids as moral agents in the world could impact the choices. Moreover, parents must balance out their decision making by considering time constraints. With jobs and schooling, familial selections are often burdened by demands on schedules. There must be other activities that the parents want their children to also participate in besides religious training. These other commitments create a type of competition of commitment.

It is easy to imagine how sporting and religious devotion could potentially conflict as it pertains to time commitments. Using the previous example, some parents could find themselves in the situation of having to decide whether to commit their child to a religious service or a sporting game or practice. In my youth, my parents, for instance, needed to decide whether to take my brother and I to baseball practice or to a midweek church service. My baseball commitments did not always interfere with religious practices. No games were scheduled on Sundays; however, the team did practice on Wednesday evenings, which competed with the weekly midweek church gathering.

The idea of time commitments related to sports and religions prompted me to conduct research (Shoemaker 2023b). To get a sense of how some people who participate in sports manage their time, I surveyed some pickleball players in 2022. This research included a broad quantitative survey asking numerous questions about equipment used, how long respondents had been playing pickleball, and their pickleball experiences. This survey was administered to pickleball players in Santa Fe, New Mexico, and on Bainbridge Island, Washington, the originating site of pickleball, as addressed in Chapter 4. In total, 142 pickleball players took the survey. About 90% of the respondents were over 50 years of age, with many already retired. These retirees typically maintained fewer familial responsibilities since their children, if they had children, were older. Additionally, employment didn't factor into the majority's consideration. This sample population, broadly speaking, had ample leisure time with which to invest. Demographically, the respondents' gender tilted to more female respondents (59%), with 41% being male respondents. The respondents were also highly educated, with 87% stating they had obtained a degree from a college or university. Figure 6.2 details the demographic information.

In addition to age, gender, and college education, the survey also asked individuals to state their religious identification. The survey gave several options like Buddhist, Muslim, Christian, Jewish, Hindu, etc., while offering "Spiritual But Not Religious," "Spiritual," and "No Religious Affiliation" as choices. Religious identity can be complicated. In the United States, about 30% of people identify as nonreligious or irreligious. Scholarship often refers to these people as "Religious Nones" since these people select the "none" option related to religious identity on surveys and census counts. Countries like China,

Pickleball Survey Results (N=142)		
	Santa Fe, NM Pickleball Respondents	**Bainbridge Island Pickleball Respondents**
Total Survey Respondents	74	68
50+ Years of Age	97%	80%
Female/Male	60/40%	58/42%
College Degree	89%	85%
Religiously Identifies	60%	70%

Figure 6.2

Sweden, and the Czech Republic maintain higher levels, with over 75% of the nation's population having no religious affiliation. These religious nones might be atheists or agnostics, but they could simply refuse to connect themselves with the options available in surveys. In other words, religious nones might still maintain some religious beliefs or practices while also choosing to not identify with a specific religious tradition. Approximately 65% of the total survey respondents indicated a religious or spiritual identification. This information does little to qualify how religiously devout any of these respondents are. The survey did not inquire how often an individual attended a religious ceremony or service or practiced an aspect of their religiosity or spirituality.

The survey, however, did include a question of whether the respondents committed more time to playing pickleball or to religious/spiritual commitments. Overwhelmingly, respondents admitted to more time in a typical week being granted to pickleball over religious/spiritual activities. In fact, 89% of respondents from Bainbridge Island and 86% of respondents from Santa Fe indicated they gave more time to pickleball. If we position religions and spiritualities along with sports within a cultural marketplace, this data indicates pickleball players in these areas are more devoted to the sport of pickleball than religious or spiritual commitments. The majority of respondents claimed to play pickleball at least three times per week with six hours per week being the average, although some indicated much more time devoted to the sport of pickleball.

There could be a variety of reasons for these responses. For instance, the geographic location might influence the results. Bainbridge Island is located within the "religious none zone," the Pacific Northwest region of the United States, which maintains some of the lowest levels of religiosity according to one Gallup poll. So, on Bainbridge Island, the survey responses might indicate more religious identity rather than religious practice. Yet, New Mexico is part of the southwest United States where 76% of the population claims to be very or moderately religious, according to the same Gallup study. Thus, even in a region where the vast majority claim higher levels of religiosity, respondents still positioned sport devotion over religious devotion as it pertained to time commitments. Potentially, regional demographics play less of a role in influencing the survey statistics. Another consideration might be health and wellbeing for those 50 years of age or older. The respondents playing pickleball in this age group are healthy enough to play pickleball at the time of the survey and maintaining health probably ranks as a high priority. No differences pertaining to gender and time commitments were revealed in the study: men and women played at similar rates. Should the same survey be conducted with the same respondents a decade from the original survey, there could be different priorities for the respondents. This is to say that the survey captured a moment in time for respondents.

The survey also included a direct question that asked respondents if pickleball was a spiritual or religious activity for them. The purpose of this question was to ascertain if respondents thought of their pickleball experiences as qualifying as a religious or spiritual practice or exercise. Interestingly, most of the respondents (69.7% on Bainbridge Island and 82.4% in Santa Fe) did *not* think of playing pickleball as a religious or spiritual activity. On the surface, most respondents demarcated religious and sporting commitments as distinctive; however, respondents were given a chance to address the question, "Have you experienced any moments of clarity, euphoria, or feeling present in your body while playing pickleball?" Several respondents offered multiple ways that playing the sport of pickleball was something other than ordinary to them. For instance, several used terms and phrases like flow state, hyper present, and enhancement to describe playing pickleball, similar to how the skateboarders in the qualitative research project described skating. Yet, others completely resisted ascribing anything special to the competitive sport of pickleball. What are we to make of these responses? First, as discussed in Chapter 2, people tend to operate within rigid categories of understanding the world. Religion and spirituality are very distinct places, practices, or activities for these people and possibly some of the respondents. Potentially, for them, sports do not qualify in this category. Second, spirituality and religiosity carry a variety of personal connotations. Some people potentially simply correlate spiritual or religious as negative descriptors. Thus, spiritual or religious labels would be inappropriate if they enjoy pickleball. Like most surveys, the responses create more questions than complete answers.

The survey shows how research with a smaller sample size attempts to quantify how one set of sporting enthusiasts (pickleball players) balance their life commitments concerning religion/spirituality. There are limitations to this type of survey project. To get a much richer picture of this topic, a larger sample size survey could be conducted. The larger number of respondents taking a survey equates to a better picture of perspectives and representation. A future, similar survey could broaden the scope of the project. For instance, an additional project could survey athletes of various sports to get comparison data. Do hockey or soccer players face similar decision making related to sports and religious devotions? Or are some sports better suited for religious devotion due to more corresponding schedules? How do social norms influence these structures? Increasingly scholars are finding a mixed methods approach to help gather more robust data. A mixed methods approach would incorporate both a quantitative angle coupled with qualitative interviews. The quantitative data would supply numerical responses to research inquiries, while the qualitative data could help fill in any questionable gaps within the numerical statistics.

BOX 6.3 QUANTITATIVE SURVEYING EXERCISE

Like the qualitative exercise in Box 6.2, quantitative research begins with a research inquiry. What question needs to be addressed for the research project? This should be narrow enough to be measurable but not so narrow that the scope hinders the project.

Quantitative research often employs surveys to address research inquiries with the intention of garnering enough survey responses to yield a representative data sample. Once the research inquiry is developed, consider what questions would best address the inquiry. Unlike qualitative interviews, which tend to be in person, quantitative survey questions need to be very clear to the wide range of respondents. Respondents will not typically be able to ask the researcher in person to clarify survey questions or word selections. For instance, in the pickleball survey, numerous people I encountered on Bainbridge Island who completed the survey were stumped by the usage of spirituality. "What did I mean by spiritual?" many asked. Researchers should consider what common terms are used by the sample population. For example, a survey would look quite different when administered to a group of scholars of religion versus a group of skateboarders. Every subgroup creates and uses its specific language. Keep this in mind. A good practice is to test your survey questions before going live with the project. Also, consider the ordering of survey questions. For instance, if the first question on a survey relates to religious affiliation, then the survey taker might assume they are answering all questions primarily based on their religious identity. Typically, demographic information is collected last in the survey.

Similar to qualitative research, the researcher must consider the sample pool. Who are the target respondents, and, importantly, how can the survey be administered to reach those respondents. There are various types of samples in quantitative studies. Using a phone bank or other resources, a random sample of people yields the purist representative data. A survey conducted randomly at different times in various spots on a university campus would create a random sample of college students. A convenience sample is often used because of limitations on time or resources. Surveying a college class would be an example of a convenience survey. This isn't representative of the entire campus but it would yield some data for consideration.

There are numerous online survey tools available to researchers. These include Google Forms and SurveyMonkey. SurveyMonkey does have a limit on the number of responses in the free edition. These surveying technologies summarize data and offer simple visuals like pie charts and graphs. This equips the researcher with rudimentary tools necessary to conduct a quantitative study. There are plenty of other options available as well. Once the survey closes, the data might need further analysis beyond what the technology supplies, which could require some statistical analysis. This can get complicated very quickly. There are numerous resources and courses available regarding how to analyze large data sets.

Like the qualitative research portion of this chapter, this is only an introduction to creating, administering, and analyzing a quantitative survey project. Nuances exist in best practices of constructing survey questions, like which survey instruments to utilize, how to

> identify sample pools, and how to convert the data into legible information. Scholars trained in social sciences offer expertise in this area and could be consulted regarding quantitative research.

CHAPTER SYNOPSIS

The main argument of this chapter is that sports and religions of all kinds of varieties directly and indirectly compete. The direct competitions signal an attempt to divert an individual's attention and resources to one specific sport or religious tradition. To fully capture someone as a "sold-out fan" means current and future commitment to the team, sport, religion, or spirituality. Indirect competition occurs when individuals consider the limited time and resources they have to invest in specific phenomena. Although some people might like to play numerous sports in leagues or at local parks, other responsibilities and time factors restrict what can be accomplished. In the pickleball example, the data shows that many pickleball players devote more time to the sport than to religious or spiritual commitments. There are bound to be individuals who devote more time to religiosity; likewise, there are people who balance their life with religious and sporting commitments. These competitions are better studied through a cultural marketplace approach, which recognizes the consumer tendencies of people and the ways global and local capitalism operates.

This chapter also highlights how qualitative and quantitative studies can aid in addressing research inquiries. Both methods provide a means of collecting data in order to discover what people are doing, why they do what they do, and how they understand what they do. Each method has its weaknesses, but each method provides a glimpse into lived realities. Hopefully, as a part of the chapter, developing scholars of religious studies and sports are inspired to build, implement, and analyze a research project so as to contribute to the growing knowledge of religions and sports. No single scholar comprehensively answers all questions related to the relationships between religions and sports; rather knowledge building on this subject, like other subjects, is dependent on a collective and collaborative approach to better understand our topic.

RECOMMENDED READING

Individuals do not think of religions operating within a competitive marketplace. This is understandable since many people think of religions or faith traditions as something uniquely different from other phenomena. However, several works demonstrate the supply and demand realities of how religions function. Torkel Brekke's (2016) *Faithonomics: Religion and the Free Market* and Larry Withham's (2010) *Marketplace of the Gods: How Economics Explains Religion* both illustrate how adopting an economic approach to understanding religion reveals the supply and demand aspects of religious practices. The religious marketplace concept is most adeptly witnessed with start-up or splintering religious groups. Thus, Rodney Stark and William Bainbridge's (1985) *The Future of Religion* focuses attention on cult and sect development through a religious marketplace lens. Combined these projects prove the value of marketplace theory in studying religious organizations, competitions, and formations.

Examining the options people have today related to spirituality, Susannah Crockford's (2021) *Ripples of the Universe* is a great analysis of the spiritual marketplace and the impact of capitalism in Sedona, Arizona. This book incorporates numerous moving pieces in her analysis of how capitalism's marketplace affects individual lives and decision making. To better understand how and why people make religious decisions, *Choosing Our Religion* by Elizabeth Drescher (2016) is a qualitative study offering numerous interview samples to uncover why people leave specific traditions while maintaining certain individual practices of that tradition. Paul Heelas and Linda Woodhead's (2005) *The Spiritual Revolution* differentiates contemporary perspectives on religion and spirituality through their mixed methods research project. Each of these works employ qualitative practices to offer on-the-ground perspectives of individuals exploring spiritual options while also citing numerous quantitative surveys so as to situate their project more broadly. To complement these works, Paul O'Connor's (2019) *Skateboarding and Religion* examines the cultural components of skateboarding as it pertains to religious dimensions.

CONCLUSION
RELIGIONS, SPORTS, AND DISRUPTIONS

The core of this book evaluates the relationships between sports and religions. In the previous chapters, five different relationships unfolded offering insights into the contours of human experience. In this last chapter, I want to first offer a review of the previous chapters. After establishing this review, the rest of the chapter focuses on what the recent COVID-19 pandemic tells us about the value of sports and religions in the contemporary world. In most places around the globe, the pandemic brought about a massive shut down of routines for individuals and societies in an attempt to slow the spread of the virus. With mass numbers of people dying across the globe, mitigating the spread of the COVID-19 virus led to shutting down day-to-day operations. Dining at restaurants, attending school sessions, and traveling in airplanes simply stopped. Online spaces supplied a means of continuing some daily patterns (i.e., school transitioned to online platforms); however, as the length of the pandemic continued, many people longed to get back to their routines.

Looking at the suspension of sports during the pandemic creates an opportunity to test some of the theories we've examined in this book, particularly around the sports as religious expression theories. In the following, I apply three early theories of religion to the suspension of sports to see how these theories might explain a human longing to participate in sport while also considering how the pandemic potentially forces us to reconsider aspects of the theoretical frameworks. Specifically, Karl

DOI: 10.4324/9781003362630-7

Marx, Rudolph Otto, and Mircea Eliade's theories provide three different approaches to understanding what constitutes religion and whether sports mimic or mirror religion in the ways these scholars propose.[1] What these scholars could not have anticipated is a global suspension of collective sport and religious practices due to a biological disruption. Thus, the suspension of sport creates an opportune time to test religious studies theories.

THE INTERSECTIONS OF SPORTS AND RELIGIONS

The first two frameworks offered within this book illustrate how sports and religions intersect. Remember, most people think of religions and sports as operating in separate and designated spaces. As most recognized religions are institutionalized, many religious communities maintain a building or space designated as such. For religious traditions, architecture reflects the values of the community. For instance, some religious communities maintain imposing buildings with large steeples pointing to the heavens as a means of recognizing the grandeur of their deity and the human devotion to that deity, while other religious traditions denounce grandeur as a wasteful or reckless way to spend the communities' finances. Thus, although there exists a wide variety of religious architecture, these buildings tend to communicate that their primary purposes are dedicated for religious purposes. Likewise, sporting facilities are built for particular sports. Whether this be an indoor gymnasium or an outdoor field or pitch, the primary purpose of these spaces is for operating a sport or game. The everyday construction of more-developed societies influences our thinking so that we compartmentalize sports from religions and vice versa.

What people notice, but are less attentive to, are the ways that sports and religions intersect in these spaces. Whether a player shows a sign of religious devotion or a religious community offers a sports recreational league, the boundaries between religions and sports are quite porous. Both the *sports in religions* and *religions in sports* frameworks compel us to pause and examine when and how the two phenomena get transmitted into various domains of life. Individual religiosity sometimes doesn't get checked at the door of a sporting arena. Athletes might offer a quiet sign of gratitude to a deity with a simple pointing to the sky or acknowledge the athletic gifts granted to them by a deity in an interview. Citing some athletes who are Muslim, we can see the differences between Muhammad Ali and Hakeem Olajuwon in how public they were about their religiosity during their professional careers. Ali tended to be quite vocal about his devotion to the Nation of Islam while Olajuwon was more reserved about fasting during Ramadan. Sports also find their way into religious spaces. With the popularity of sports, some religious communities operate sporting leagues as a means of recruiting new members or developing the character of existing members. At other times, some athletes utilize sports as a means of social acceptance due to barriers caused by discrimination toward their religiosity. The examples covered in these chapters, although merely the tip of the iceberg, demonstrate the intersectional elements of sports and religions.

What these examples inevitably produce are discussions of whether athletes *should* express their religiosity within sporting spaces or if religious communities *should* adopt and operate sporting leagues. This will certainly depend on cultural norms and vary from society to society. Social norms and legal structures regarding religions inform many opinions on this question. Although there is a spectrum of secular positions, some secular societies might frown upon religious expression in public sporting events. In certain countries with religious legal codes recognizing only specific forms of religiosity, these issues grow much more complex. On an individual level, some religious athletes might understand their religiosity as a key aspect of life, not restricted to specific religious rituals or events; but not all fans might share the same position in this regard. With different opinions and attitudes toward religious expressions in sporting spaces or sports leagues within religious spaces, the controversy embedded in the question demonstrates the value many people ascribe to these identities and phenomena. Sports and religiosity are serious issues for many devotees. A situation wherein individuals are limited in their sports or religious participation would cause a severe disruption to people's routines and habits.

THE INTERACTIONS OF SPORTS AND RELIGIONS

In addition to the intersectional approach to studying religions and sports, this book also analyzes the interactive aspects of religions and sports. This is demonstrated in two different, but complementary ways. First, religions and sports in dialogue illustrates how religious leaders and athletes sometimes embrace the opportunity to collaborate to achieve shared goals. The example of the Pope discussing racial issues with NBA players exhibits one case study in which representatives from a large religious tradition (Catholicism) and a popular sporting league (the NBA) took the time to discuss a social ill – systemic racism – plaguing societies across the globe. Listening to the experiences of black professional athletes combined with hearing about the activism of NBA players, the Pope and other Catholic leaders might be better prepared to engage racism within the Catholic churches' organization and within parishes across the globe. This teaches or reminds us that sports and religions exist within the same social circumstances. Racism is not restricted to policing or hiring practices but permeates all of society including religious organizations and sporting leagues.

Second, because religions and sports operate in the daily lives of individuals, there is bound to be competition between religious and sporting options. With a plethora of choices attracting members of society as consumers, individuals must make decisions regarding where they will give their attention and time. For a person who is either a religious devotee or a sports fan, but not both, this might make choosing easier. For the person who identifies with both religious affiliation and sporting fandom, choices can get complicated by a limited amount of time to invest in both of these phenomena. This competitive aspect of religions and sports positions both phenomena within a vast market of options wherein the individual consumer must determine their preferences. Can individuals balance both sports fandom and religious devotion? Of course. However, might there be times when the individual must make an either/or decision due to time restraints? Certainly. Hundreds of other consumer options crowd the decision-making processes. Furthermore, the competition between sports and religions might be direct or indirect.

The competitive and collaborative interactions of sports and religions illustrate the value added of both religious commitment and sporting fandoms or participation. The dialogue shows the power that athletes and religious leaders have to address specific social situations. These voices emerge during the pandemic offering critiques or advice emphasizing the important role people ascribe to athletes and religious leaders. The competitive interactions between sports and religions display two consumer choices of profound importance: sports and religions hold a significant place in the cultural marketplace of options. A disruption in the cultural market would substantially alter people's practices and activities. In sum, sports and religions constitute a social power that attracts millions of people across the world.

THE MIMETIC NATURE OF SPORTS AND RELIGIONS

Although the intersectional and interactive nature of sports and religions certainly advances many of the ways in which these two phenomena engage, the mimetic nature of religions and sports proposes family resemblances so deeply entrenched that some argue sports are similar to religious activity. When analyzing how sports operate and function in societies across the globe, the correlative kinship of sports and religions cannot be denied. Some scholars advocate that this kinship exists as a mirroring effect: sports mirror much of what religion does. Whereas religions offer individuals and collectives the opportunity to participate in rituals and symbolic meaning making, sports do the same. Wearing a favorite jersey with a superstitious belief that this will aid in a team winning echoes religious rituals presupposing an outcome based on the ritual. These types of ritual activities supply humans a means of imagining that they are contributing to a desired outcome, whether this is actually the case or not. Sports fans find deep meaning in these activities, particularly when others share in the rituals. This forms a collective working together to affect sporting outcomes. In this argument, sports are like religions, but religious activities are still different in essence from sporting activities.

To take the argument further, some scholars argue that sports constitute religious activity. These types of arguments typically build from theories of secularism and *homo religiosus*. The former, secularism, supposes a gradual decline of commitments to religious authority. As science continues to advance technologically, people might find religion obsolete. However, humans still require religious outlets due to the *homo religiosus* argument supposing humans are essentially religious beings. From this perspective, even though a general trend away from religious authority might be developing in some countries around the globe, these humans still need a means of channeling their inner religious needs. Thus, sports displace religions. The rituals, meaning making, and belief systems embedded in sports do mirror religiosity, but this is true because sports are the new religion. Sports fans are religious beings practicing religiosity.

Whether one adopts the sports mirror religions or the sports constitute religious activity theories, both of them build from a notion that religions form an intense level of meaning and vitality to the human experience; and, thus, sports functionally mirror that level of intensity. If religion creates some of the most heightened, and often fierce, commitments, and if sports are similar in magnitude, then these commitments demonstrate the importance of religions and sports for humans. If a global pandemic interrupts these commitments, the effects could be devastating to the humans devoted to the institutions and organizations operating religious and sporting events, practices, and opportunities. A key aspect of individual routines could be upended with the need to isolate from other humans during a calamitous pandemic.

> **BOX 7.1 FRAMEWORK COMPARISONS AND INNOVATIONS**
>
> Summarizing the five frameworks utilized in this book creates a moment to compare the different approaches to understanding and analyzing the intersections, interactions, and mirroring aspects of religions and sports. The intersectional framework relies on the notion that individuals maintain multiple identities, and that these

identities are not restricted to specific spaces. So, a religious athlete's religious identity can emerge in spaces prioritizing the athlete's sports identity. Likewise, sports identities can be located within some religious spaces. The interactive framework highlights the discourse occurring between religious and sporting elites. With the social power connected to contemporary religious and sporting institutions, religious leaders and professional athletes and coaches embrace a societal pulpit to articulate perspectives on social issues. Last, the mirroring aspects of religions and sports cast a spotlight on the intense devotion people apply to these cultural phenomena. Time, finances, and energy directed to religious and sporting activities provide people with a tremendous sense of life satisfaction and wellbeing.

As religions and sports develop in a fast-paced global society, a need arises to analyze the continued usefulness of these frameworks. In other words, are there social circumstances drastically or slightly altering religious and sporting phenomena? Are these changes in national or local contexts reducing the effectiveness of these frameworks? As an exercise, take time to consider some of the latest trends, activities, or circumstances in specific locations that could alter the relationship between religions and sports. For instance:

- Do some changes in government structures limit religious or sporting activities in certain regions of the world?
- As capitalism drives much of the decision making across the globe, and forms counter responses to the dominance of capitalism, are there changes adjusting interactions of sports and religions?
- Where are specific religions growing or declining? Does this affect the sports industry?
- Where are interests in specific sports increasing or declining? Does this affect religious institutions or personal religiosity?

In considering these questions, the reader might consider the contemporary situations and factors forcing change in the world. As these circumstances alter human lives across the globe or in locales, daily routines might be disrupted. Are these disruptions positive or negative for religions and sports? Furthermore, as humanity continues to evolve, the provided frameworks could lose

> their value for studying sports and religions. Take a moment to consider which frameworks are the most stable or unstable. With an increase of those disaffiliating in certain countries, does this reduce the ability of religious leaders to interactively engage with athletes to address social ills? On the opposite end, in countries where religion is growing, does this impact the ability of certain religious leaders to speak out on morals, ethics, and issues, and are there instances where these leaders attempt to partner with athletes? What do these situations look like? How might technological advancements disrupt the value of religions and sports for some individuals?
>
> As social and individual advancement progresses, we might need to admit that a framework loses its effectiveness. Since social science advances with human development, we would simply ask: what other frameworks are needed to adequately analyze sports and religions? Admittedly, this is an introduction to the relationships between religions and sports and the case studies included in this book cannot possibly consider all sports and religions in all locations at all times. Can the reader think of another framework to complement or improve upon the frameworks included in the preceding chapters? What does this approach look like? How would a new approach be similar or dissimilar from the five frames of this work?

ON HUMAN DISTRACTIONS

An important part of the human experience is spent developing societies' structures, activities, legal systems, and operations. The structures existing today are the result of hundreds, if not thousands, of years of formation. Values such as efficiency and efficacy, along with necessity, drive the human compulsion to improve, extend, or better life's circumstances. Manipulating the environment, building safety structures, and ensuring access to food all encompass much of what ancient humans focused their attention on. As societies developed, and security increased to protect humans from outside forces, humans developed time to consider life's bigger questions while also making time for leisure pursuits. Generally speaking, cultural pursuits of play and thinking about life's bigger questions related to death, human existence, and human origins are found in most cultures historically. These pursuits formed the basis of religions and sports today.

An important part of human history, unfortunately, are disruptions to human attempts to organize life. Wars and famines wreak havoc in various times causing those humans to contend with what to do in particular moments. Some scholars like Peter Berger (1967) argue that the disruptions in life create the need for religions to develop as a "sacred canopy." The sacred canopy supplies reasons for disruptions to life, granting humans a reason to continue on even when life is quite bleak. Why did our community suffer dramatically through a dry season with no harvest yield this year? Without scientific explanations, some might invent the retaliation or punishment of a deity upon the society as a cause. As Berger posits:

> [Religion] permits the individual who goes through [life disruptions] to continue to exist in the world of his society – not "as if nothing had happened," which is psychologically difficult in the more extreme marginal situations, but in the "knowledge" that even these events or experiences have a place within a universe that makes sense.
>
> (p. 44)

This could provoke the society to invent rituals in order to placate that deity from imposing future droughts. At the same time, during some disruptions, humans took the time to continue playing. Difficult situations must be engaged, but playing can offer a reprieve from the seriousness of life granting physical, emotional, and mental improvement.

In modern history, examples demonstrate that sometimes humans have made the decision to cancel certain practices in order to address more pressing issues. Immediately following the events of September 11, 2001 in the United States, sports were temporarily canceled. Likewise, the 1944 Summer Olympics were canceled due to the major world war occurring at that time. In 2020, a global virus emerged disrupting social life for billions of people across the planet; COVID-19, an infectious disease, required social distancing to slow transmission rates. At the time of this writing, the World Health Organization estimates approximately 6.9 million deaths due to the COVID-19 infection. As millions of people died from the virus, sports and religious gatherings simply came to a screeching stop beginning in 2020. Several academic studies approach various aspects of the lack of sports during the pandemic (Glebova et al. 2022; Grix et al. 2020; Mann et al. 2020; Westmattelmann et al. 2020). These studies explore the safety measures imposed once athletes return to competition, the role of virtual spectatorship during the pandemic, and how COVID-19 impacted sports in general. One study highlights the differential impacts of the loss of sports on various social classes and a greater need for local sporting opportunities (Grix et al. 2020). This correlates, again, with Berger's analysis of society: "there are events affecting entire societies or social groups that provide massive threats to the reality previously taken for granted" (p. 44). Sports, and religions, constitute part of the taken-for-granted reality that many people rely on as key aspects of their life patterns. During the pandemic, sports were simply suspended until medical professionals announced that it was safe to return to social events.

Unlike Berger, who thinks religions are a key part of human life, Karl Marx (1970) argues that religions are an invented distraction to keep the general population from revolution during times of drastic economic, political, and material inequalities. Since Marx's primary question revolved around inequalities and the redistribution of material wealth, religions, from Marx's perspective, created an interference for revolting against unjust distribution of resources. Marx famously called religion "the opiate of the masses," keeping people placated with ideas about an improved afterlife or reasons for inequalities related to supernatural design. Importantly, it's not simply that religions function as a coping mechanism in Marx's argument, but that the bourgeois, the class of business owners and elite politicians who control wealth, use religions as a political tool to keep the current distribution of wealth intact. In other words, if people are promised a better afterlife if they suffer through the conditions in this world then they tend to rebel less. For a political philosopher intent on redistributing material wealth, it is easy to imagine that Marx understood religion as an impediment to the political work needed to be conducted in this life. Like religion, other cultural phenomena such as literature and art could also function to distract people.

Scholars, using Marx's idea, debate whether sports operate as a means of placating the masses, much like religion, or if sports offer a beneficial time of leisure and rest. Richard Giulianotti (2005) expresses this both/and perspective of Marx: "Bourgeois-controlled sport must be interpreted as a regressive and ideological force," but "only a communist revolution would negate [sport's] commodification and alienation" providing a needed outlet for workers (p. 64). Under oppressive circumstances, sport creates the opiate effect that distracts workers from tackling the pressing concerns of unequal distribution of goods; however, in egalitarian societies, workers could utilize sport and leisure for pleasure. Sports, from a Marxist position, can either be a meaningful and recuperative activity for those who play and spectate or an aspect of a broader system of political control. Eric Bain-Selbo and Gregory Sapp (2016) employ a Marxist application to analyzing sports. They admit a negative valuation of sports as it pertains to diverting attention away from important issues like race and class matters. They argue, "[Sport] provides us an escapist path to an illusory world, preventing us from genuinely engaging reality and thus stopping us from addressing injustices and changing the world for the better" (p. 115). Moreover, "While providing some measure of equal opportunity for all, sport paradoxically conceals and reveals the underlying injustices of society...[Sport] is increasingly becoming the new 'opiate of the masses'" (p. 122). Similar to Marx's critique of religion, sport, according to Bain-Selbo and Sapp, redirects sports fans' attention away from reality where wealth and racial inequalities exist.

The COVID-19 suspension of sports supplies a moment to pause and appraise the value of sports in the contemporary world. First, Bain-Selbo and Sapp certainly make a good argument that during typical days (i.e., when people worry less about pandemics and personal health), sports, compared to addressing systemic issues like social and racial inequalities, are a cultural diversion. However, the results of the COVID-19 pandemic reveal a positive contribution of sports as a distracting force. The pandemic, broadly speaking, brought human vulnerability to the surface and leveled inaccessibility to many cultural luxuries and comforts. With most leisure and cultural activities temporarily canceled, coupled with the stressors of the pandemic (illness, death, and the unknown specifics of the virus), people were confronted with the banality of life. In other words, people, confronted with boredom, longed for a distraction from the daily news of the growing pandemic, stressful health updates from friends and family members, and the monotony of in-home activities.

Before the pandemic outbreak, I concluded from my research that sports offered a necessary distraction in another way. My research project (Shoemaker 2019) focused on those who had decided to leave their family's conservative (and often very rigid) Christian faith tradition. Parents within these conservative religious communities maintained the expectation that their offspring, even in adulthood, would follow in their footsteps and continue to hold similar beliefs and practices. This decision to move away from the family's faith community led to arguments and conflicts within the family. During my interviews, I asked questions regarding what life was like with family members after leaving the family's religious community, and, unexpectedly at that time, many of my interviewees stated that shared sports fandom was the one activity allowing the family members to set aside political and religious differences. While watching their favorite basketball or football teams, my interviewees explained that all other matters temporarily vanished, and the family could set aside differences. Their shared fandom trumped, at least momentarily, different worldviews; or stated differently, sports created a healthy distraction from the pressing fissures dividing members of the family.

Marx's assessment of religion and other cultural phenomena as an "opiate of the masses" typically gets read from a negative perspective. Certainly, Marx meant it as such. Religion interferes with immediate concerns and generally with social ills that need rectifying. Likewise, similar evaluations of sports contend the same. However, humans are more than workers focused on material comforts. The pandemic reveals a need for healthy distractions from overwhelmingly troublesome moments in human history. To get back to the "previously taken for granted reality," as Berger suggests, highlights the need for sports and religions for people around the globe. Both sports and religions create the opportunity to focus attention elsewhere when pressing concerns compound individual and collective thoughts. Sports rituals and gatherings, like religious rituals and gatherings, offer safer spaces for mental and emotional recovery during particularly onerous times. The opiate effect could be humanity's attempt to cope with the often-harsh realities of life.

ON HUMAN TIME STRUCTURING

Historically, humans devised creative ways to structure concepts of time. Using star patterns and nature's seasons, our ancestors computed day lengths and established calendar systems. As part of the devised calendars, tribes and societies designated certain days, months, or even years as special or unique. Religions commonly served as the mediator of these sacred holy times, attaching rituals and events to mark occasions. In societies around the globe, religious institutions continue to manage calendars, oversee ritual activities, and organize festivals. Related to the topic of time structures, Mircea Eliade (1959), referenced in the fourth chapter, analyzed ritual activities around the globe, and found cultures that organize annual festivals, establish liturgical calendars, and re-enact divine myths constituting a sacred time, which is essentially different than mundane time. Humans need to transcend what Eliade calls "the historical present," through a recurring calendar of rituals expressed through religious rites and events (p. 70).

Joseph L. Price (2001) applies Eliade's theoretical frameworks to the relationship among sacred time, place, and sport in his book, *From Season to Season*. Price's argument hinges on the idea that various sports calendars order time in contemporary societies, similar to what liturgical calendars do for religious communities. This obviously doesn't apply to every society across the globe, but does in secularizing societies with no shared religious affiliation or rituals. As some societies move toward secularization, people still need ways to structure time and connect themselves to their world. According to Price: "Like most religious calendars, the primary function of the American sports calendar is to provide some kind of ritual transition from the chaos of secularity to the cosmos of sports, from cultural malaise to corporate hope" (p. 57). Ordinary time is mundane; sacred time is extraordinary and enchanted with mystery and hope. Sacred time grants people something to look forward to while also overtly or subversively corresponding with other natural seasons.

Many modern fans organize their personal calendars around sporting schedules like opening days, regular season play, and tournaments. These sporting calendars tend to align with the natural weather cycles of specific locations. When spring training starts, baseball fans energetically anticipate the opportunity to analyze their team's chances in the upcoming season, but spring training also indicates the closing of winter months in the United States with spring approaching. Many basketball fans anticipate the summer season toward the end of the NBA playoffs. As cooler weather approaches and summer heat begins to fade, fans instinctively know the American football season is around the corner. Student and amateur athletes correlate seasonal activities with sporting opportunities. Runners anticipate participating in races recurring on the same weekend in a specific month each year. In each of these examples, athletes and fans connect through shared commitments to time. The rhythm of sporting seasons outlines time for fans and athletes – an integral aspect to an overall rhythmic excitement filling the mundane with energy and anticipation. Communication scholar Michael Serazio (2019) summarizes these sentiments:

> Above all, sport tells us what time it is. Its temporal quality is essential to its cultural power: the ability to anchor participants (players and fans alike) in the present moment; to concentrate a vast, shared psychic energy on events unfolding before us right now. It orients observers; synchronizes schedules; coordinates collectivity.
>
> (p. 30)

Sports, in sum, provide reference points for the temporal nature of human life.

The need to suspend collective events, during the COVID-19 pandemic, created unstructured timelines and schedules lacking the normal tracking of time. One study found that for athletes a serious difficulty during the pandemic was the "total uncertainty, both in terms of future events and in terms of preparation, which makes it difficult to maintain motivation" (Glebova et al. 2022, p. 61). With the unavailability of definite time structures, many athletes simply lost motivation. This also plagued sports fans as well. The period of sporting absence brought about a stalling of time without shared rituals to enact our human calendars. With the COVID-19 pandemic and absence of sports, we could say that, anthropologically and sociologically, many people might lose track of *who* they are because they do not know *when* they are. A key aspect of sports, often overlooked, are scheduled moments – events marking special, sacred occasions. Without the accustomed sporting events, athletes and fans alike experience the mundane, marked with little significance.

Some people might not consider themselves sports fans, however non-sports fans are still informed by sporting seasons. Take for instance, the example that non-football fans participate in the NFL's Super Bowl events due to gathering friends and family around food and spectatorship. Like the Christian holy days of Easter and Christmas serving as calendared events for Christians and non-Christians alike, sports serve the community in organizing calendars. The temporary disruption of sports creates a void in the timekeeping mechanisms of societies across the globe and gives a glimpse into just how essential cultural expressions are to calendaring modern life.

BOX 7.2 CALENDARS AND SCHEDULES

Although there might be a universality to structuring time through rituals and specially-designated events and activities, the specifics of these events, days, and rituals are quite unique across the globe. Each locale develops ways of being to separate themselves from others and form a uniqueness. For example, although most societies celebrate a New Year's festival or ritual, these vary drastically. For this exercise, we will be thinking about the rituals normalized in the reader's community or society.

Anthropologist Horace Miner (1956) wrote a piece titled, "Body Ritual Among the Nacirema." In his work, he studies the odd morning ritual exercises conducted by a large society of people. The purposes of these daily rituals prepare the individual to meet social expectations and include applying magic charms and a mouth-rite. The mouth-rite includes "inserting a small bundle of hog-hairs into the mouth, along with certain magical powders, and then moving the bundle in a highly formalized series of gestures" (p. 504). Miner describes other rituals that might sound odd to an outsider but indicate that these people find the human body less than desirable in its current state. Thus, the rituals are attempts at improving the human body for social interactions. I highly recommend reading Miner's anthropological findings for yourself.

We might read Miner's descriptions of activities and be quite confused about this group and their ritual practices. However, one point Miner drives home is that all rituals are foreign to those outside the community practicing the rituals. In fact, Miner's work actually details brushing one's teeth and visiting a dentist for professional teeth cleaning (a.k.a. mouth-rites). Nacirema is simply American spelled backwards. Consider how odd it must be for some individuals to hear about the daily grooming rituals of Americans who tend to pride themselves on outward appearance. Shaving, bathing, brushing teeth, or applying perfume or cologne might seem obvious to those in the United States or in similar countries sharing these practices, but the time devoted to one's physical appearance might seem like a waste of time or simply unusual to those who place less emphasis on these matters.

Just as Miner reflected on the rituals of his own society, let's take time to reflect on the rituals of the reader's society. How would you respond to the following prompts?

Daily: Miner's paper focuses on the daily rituals of life. Take a moment to consider what daily rituals you participate in. Where and when do these rituals take place? How are the rituals conducted? Who is allowed to participate and who is disallowed? How might you measure the necessity of these rituals (absolutely necessary or inconsequential)?

Monthly or Annually: Broadening out the timeline, what monthly or annual rituals do you enact? Are there specially designated events, festivals, or gatherings that create an eager anticipation? The same set of questions as before can examine these rituals: When and where? How? Who? Value?

> **Social:** What events take place in or near your community. Maybe you participate or choose not to. Either way, who participates? How many people participate in these activities? What's the purpose? Is there typically a subgroup of people who enact these activities? Who plans and organizes these events? Do these events align with a change in natural seasons? What resources are used in the event?
>
> Now imagine these events simply stop with no warning or announcement. Who is left disappointed with the ceasing of these events? What, if anything, is lost? Could an alternative event take the place of the original event? Maybe take the time to set up a conversation with someone who participates to ask them what the event means to them.

ON HUMAN GATHERING AND SPECTATORSHIP

Gathering together collectively is a vital part of the human experience. Over the course of human history, social gatherings provide a time of connection, support, and strategizing. Reasons for gatherings range from political, ritualistic, and entertainment. Some of the largest gatherings in history revolve around either religious or sporting events. For instance, in 2015, an estimated six million people attended a Mass conducted by Pope Francis in the Philippines. With Catholicism being the largest branch of Christianity based on the number of adherents, Filipinos took the opportunity to hear their religious leader live during the Feast of Santo Niño. Or consider the crowds of fans who gathered in 2022 to welcome home the FIFA World Cup champions, Argentina's national football team. Approximately five million people spectated as their beloved team paraded down the streets of Buenos Aires. We could recount several other historical and contemporary examples of mass human gatherings centering on religious and sporting devotion.

A key element of these gatherings is the ability to witness, first-hand, the event. Spectators hope to catch a glimpse of their religious leaders or professional athletes while sharing in the emotional energy generated by others sharing similar interests. Emile Durkheim (1912), an early sociologist, theorized that within religious gatherings participants experience "collective effervesce," a unified energy among the participants. Within these gatherings, "feelings of joy, inner peace, serenity, and enthusiasm that, for the faithful, stand as experimental proof of their beliefs" (p. 420). Although science lags behind in trying to measure the forces at play when humans gather together for unified, peaceful purposes, Durkheim recognizes the energy instantiated in such events. Durkheim's theory can easily be applied to sports (Grix et al. 2020; Bain-Selbo and Sapp 2016). Jonathan Grix and his team of scholars detail the ways sports provides a means of collective effervescence:

> Many sports fans experience 'collective effervescence' through regular live sporting consumption, in particular, at weekly football matches around which their lives are constructed: weekend (and occasionally mid-week) sports matches involve the build up to the game in the week prior to the game, pre-meetings on match day with other fans, often in a social setting (pub or bar), the match itself where the collective experience is undertaken and then the post-event analysis which may take several days, before the cycle begins again. It will also be at such events that the 'feelgood' factor is at its highest for the home fans, sharing, chanting, booing and whistling.
>
> (p. 4)

The constitution of sporting events allows fans to become part of the activity, sharing with the athletes. At these moments, an extraordinary connection exists between the fans, athletes, coaches, and the sport itself.

What happens when these moments are removed from society due to health concerns? The COVID-19 pandemic required social distancing to reduce the transmission of deadly and debilitating pathogens. For good reasons, human gatherings came to an abrupt halt. Some individuals tailored their work habits so as to lessen interactions or created offices to work from home. Religious gatherings, like other activities, were either canceled, delayed, or transitioned to online platforms. Most sporting events postponed practices and events for the protection of athletes in sports requiring close proximity of play. Likewise, concerts and other live events were postponed.

Knowing devoted fans would miss live sports and that athletes respond to fans' support when playing, some sporting organizations made an effort to supply alternatives. During the pandemic, a limited number of sporting events were made available online and through television. The NBA and WNBA maintained a "bubble" for their players, keeping them isolated and monitored their health with daily COVID-19 tests. During the basketball game broadcasts, some fans were given the opportunity to "attend" the game with monitors showing the virtual spectators. Some baseball games prohibited in-person attendance, but cardboard cutouts showed fans in seats with artificial sound effects of cheers and boos. These attempts at filling the spectator gaps failed to meet the experience of attending the games live or even watching the games with close friends and family members. At other moments, some television stations simply re-aired previous matches and games. For example, CBS ran previously played and recorded NCAA basketball tournament games when trying to replace the canceled men's' March Madness tournament. These replays, reruns, proxy fans, and virtual fandoms attempted to fill a sporting void when live games were suspended.

Rudolph Otto's (1958) and William James' (1982) work regarding religious experience provides some insight into why this is the case. Otto concentrated on religious experience, not as a tradition or institution, but as an intense experience that dramatically affects the individual. According to Otto, these religious experiences are ineffable, and the emotions derived from the experience cannot be duplicated through human engineering. Religion then "must be experienced in oneself to be understood" (p. 10). Religious institutions and traditions emerge as an attempt to duplicate or recreate the initial religious experience of specific individuals. Likewise, William James defined religion as an experience that altered peoples' life trajectories. These deeply meaningful experiences cannot be humanly fabricated in worship services or formalized rituals, which are of a second order, but religious experiences are spontaneous first-hand experiences. James proposes, "We must search rather for the original experience which were the pattern-setters" (p. 6). Religious experiences, according to both Otto and James, are irreplicable moments in human life because they are utterly unique.

Otto and James supply us with a way of thinking about an ordering of human experiences. Applied to aspects of religion, direct experience supersedes any attempt to recapture the initial event. These ideas can be applied more broadly to sporting events and offer an explanation of why the replayed and virtual fandoms failed to meet up to the live, in-person spectating. Spectating a live sporting event is a first-order experience; replaying sporting events, with all of its benefits, is of a second-order – it is not the actual experience. The live version includes the emotions of anticipation surrounding victory and defeat, as well as the mystery around the outcome of the game. Yet, there is something about human nature that seeks to duplicate these experiences, as if that moment could be recaptured. Sports reruns and virtual fandoms simply do not meet the level of expectation that the live and in-person experience offers. Both Otto and James supply a phenomenological insight into trying to readminister a first-order experience. During the pandemic, first-order experiences were primarily unavailable. Being separated from fellow fans without the option to spectate together or at a live event, created second-order experiences at best. This failed to adequately fulfill the human need for first-order sporting experiences.

BOX 7.3 PANDEMIC REFLECTION

In 2020, two colleagues of mine at Arizona State University developed an opportunity for people to catalog their life experiences at various times during the pandemic. These historians produced "The Journal of the Plague Year," an open-source website allowing individuals to upload photos, videos, links, and stories to an online archive resource. Thousands of contributions paint a bleak picture of life without common toiletries, access to certain groceries, and the loneliness of isolation. Contributors detailed their fears about loved ones who tested positive for COVID-19, and, sadly, recounted the loss of friends and family members. The archive remains online and open for contributions.[2] Additionally, anyone can search the archive for specific topics.

The pandemic period formed a shared human experience. Although there certainly were differences in security, comfort, and access to medical resources during the pandemic, most people maintained social distancing and isolation, creating a common event between humans across the globe. This resulted in wide-spread boredom. Recent research indicates a universality to the boredom experienced during lockdown protocols (although this varies depending on the nation state, gender, age, degree of susceptibility to disease, etc.) In one study (Wessels et al. 2022) focusing on Germany during the pandemic, scholars discovered, "respondents first indicated a considerably slowed down PPT (perceived passage of time) and increased levels of boredom than before the pandemic" (p. 8). Another study (Boateng et al. 2021) analyzing Ghanaians' experiences found increases in generalized anxiety disorders and a significant drop in reported well-being. Another medical study (Yan et al. 2021) analyzing life in China during the pandemic concluded, "individuals with a propensity to experience boredom were more likely to report greater emotional distress" (p. 6). In sum, the basic needs to be active, social, and carrying out routines, all shutdown during the pandemic, caused a massive disruption to life and resulted in negative emotional and mental consequences.

Although there are shared commonalities during the pandemic, every individual experienced life differently during the pandemic. We all interacted with different levels of loss, fear, and insecurity. We all engaged with boredom differently. In this exercise, take a moment to consider the following questions about life during the pandemic from your perspective.

- What was life generally like?
- What was time like during the pandemic? Did time move more slowly?
- Did you experience boredom? What kept you occupied?
- What were the most impactful disruptions of events for you?
- Did you miss sporting events? If so, which ones?
- Were you able to find a new playful activity to occupy time?
- Did you miss sports activities or spectating? Why?
- Did you interact with religion or spirituality? If so, how?
- Did religious activities adjust during the pandemic or simply halt? If there was an adjustment, what did the adjustment look like?
- Did religious devotion increase or decrease? Why?
- Generally speaking, what did the pandemic period teach you about what's valuable in life?

THE DYNAMIC AND ADAPTABLE NATURE OF RELIGIONS AND SPORTS

As detailed in the previous sections, religions and sports supply more than mere entertainment for those who participate. These cultural phenomena supply a way to order human life. Liturgical calendars, along with sporting calendars, provide a means to correspond human activity with nature's seasons. These rituals, festivals, and events often work subversively to arrange individual and collective schedules producing hope, anticipation, and renewal. Although Eliade focused his attention on religious rituals and calendars, sports contribute to the ordering of time in the contemporary world for individuals and societies. Since much of the everyday aspects of human life centers on labor, sports and religions form organized methods for leisure activities; yet, these activities also furnish mechanisms to cope through the uglier realities of life. Although Marx negatively assessed the opiate effect, the opiate effects of sports and religions equip humans to overlook negative circumstances, even if only temporarily. Admittedly, if religions and sports divert attention away from engaging with social ills permanently, then we might tend to agree with Marx. Additionally, first-order experiences constitute events or encounters transcending the ordinary being full of mystery and energy. Whether these are individual experiences or Durkheimian experiences of collective effervescence, people tend to describe these events as somehow special or beyond the everyday. Suspending these important human constructs of life shows the inherent value ascribed to these phenomena. The COVID-19 pandemic brings the importance into relief clearly.

What the suspension of sports and religions during the pandemic also highlights, however, is the instability of cultural phenomena. Although people might like to imagine that their religious community or favorite sports team will exist in perpetuity, the dreadfulness of the pandemic illustrates the fragility of human activity and creation. Religions and sports fit into what Peter Berger (1967) refers to as "world construction" and "world maintenance" (pp. 1–28). The world, or the organized societies humans construct, brings about order in the midst of chaos. The ordering of society systematizes daily life into a routine and pattern delivering an imagined cohesion to all of reality. The order is prone to chaos, however, including wars, disease, and death, making "all socially constructed worlds... inherently precarious" (p. 29). The precarity of life and human ordering, on full display during the pandemic, illustrates the delicate nature of sports and religions. In short, sports and religions depend upon human interest and availability to continue.

Throughout modernity, the assumption of much scholarship was that religions would disappear as science and technology advanced. This formed a foundation for the secularization thesis: science and reason would simply displace religious devotion since science and reason offered answers and solutions to human problems. In the past, humans offered prayers and small sacrifices as a means of producing good health; since science offers vaccinations and other resources to eradicate certain diseases, why would humans continue to rely on religious practices? Nevertheless, people across the globe both depend on scientific advancements *and* religious practices as emotional, mental, and physical health resources. Religion did not disappear, it merely adapted. Obviously, examples do exist of individuals abandoning religious practices for evidence-based scientific discoveries. Likewise, there are individuals who reject modern science and choose instead to rely on religious rituals. However, for many people religion and science are not an either/or option but a both/and integration. To use Berger's framework, science and religions constitute key parts of human world-construction and the maintenance of those worlds.

Although Berger argues that religions supply "sacred canopies" generating explanations for the worst aspects of human life (e.g. war, famine, death), religions might only be a segment of the canopy. We might imagine the sacred canopy as woven together elements of human world-building and maintenance helping humans push through difficult moments, like during the COVID-19 pandemic. Science definitely composes part of the sacred canopy. Scientific explanations afford rational solutions to human questions and problems permitting humans the opportunity to "continue to exist in the world of his society" (p. 44). In addition to science and religions, sports and play constitute a key part of the sacred canopy for human life. Leisure activities balance the seriousness and solemnity of existence. Even in the midst of death, humans often find the time to play. Even though large-scale sporting events, like the Olympics, might be suspended during war or pandemics, individuals still found ways to play and exercise. Like other transitions to online platforms, individuals found esports as a playful outlet during the pandemic. One team of scholars discovered that esports provide interaction and community-based interactions, a distraction from the harsh realities of the pandemic, and incorporated the "cultural symbols and rituals" of traditional sports (Pu et al. 2021, p. 12). In brief, sports adapted to pandemic circumstances while still providing elements of a sacred canopy. The sacred canopy of human life is a patchwork of cultural features.

In conclusion, religions and sports are unstable in their current forms yet dynamically adaptable to the needs and desires of the humans who construct them. Although a variety of external forces might interrupt human efforts to engage in sporting and religious maintenance, humans figure out ways to adjust these two profound cultural phenomena. Both supply reasons to continue existing even when sports and religions are "forever threatened by the forces of chaos" (Berger 1967, p. 80). The examples and approaches explicated in this book reveal the sacred qualities and characteristics of sports and religions for humans across the globe. Understanding that these two vital phenomena intersect, mimic, and interact helps to gauge how humans think about these phenomena and the ascribed necessity in maintaining them.

NOTES

1 I discuss these ideas further in a chapter contribution titled "Sport, Religion, and Absence: The Subfield of Religion and Sport as an Explanatory Tool for the Moment," in Jeffrey Scholes and Randall Balmer's edited collection, *Religion and Sports in North America: Critical Essays for the Twenty-First Century* (Shoemaker 2023a).
2 Visit https://covid-19archive.org/s/archive/page/Share

BIBLIOGRAPHY

Alpert, Rebecca. 2015. *Religion and Sports: An Introduction and Case Studies*. New York, NY: Columbia University Press.

Alpert, Rebecca. 2014. "The Macho-Mensch: Modeling American Jewish Masculinity and the Heroes of Baseball," in *Muscling in the New Worlds: Jews, Sports, and the Making of the Americas* edited by Raanan Rein and David M.K. Sheinin. Boston, MA: Brill.

Alpert, Rebecca and Arthur Remillard. 2019. *Gods, Games, and Globalization: New Perspectives on Religion and Sport*. Macon, GA: Mercer University Press.

Andersen, Marie, Laila Ottesen, and Lone Friis Thing. 2019. "The Social and Psychological Health Outcomes of Team Sport Participation in Adults: An Integrative Review of Research." *Scandinavian Journal of Public Health* 47 (8): 832–850.

Anderson, Mia Long, editor. 2023. *Social Justice and the Modern Athlete: Exploring the Role of Athlete Activism in Social Change*. New York, NY: Lexington Books.

Bain-Selbo, Eric. 2009. *Game Day and God: Football, Faith, and Politics in the American South*. Macon, GA: Mercer University Press.

Bain-Selbo, Eric and D. Gregory Sapp. 2016. *Understanding Sport as a Religious Phenomenon*. New York, NY: Bloomsbury.

Bebbington, David. 1989. *Evangelicalism in Modern Britain: A History from the 1730s to the 1980s*. London and New York, NY: Routledge.

Berger, Peter. 1967. *The Sacred Canopy: Elements of a Sociological Theory of Religion*. New York, NY: Anchor Books.

Bielo, James. 2015. *Anthropology of Religion: The Basics*. New York, NY: Routledge.

Billings, Andrew C., Leigh M. Moscowitz, Coral Rae, and Natalie Brown-Devlin. 2015. "The Art of Coming Out: Traditional and

Social Media Frames Surrounding the NBA's Jason Collins," *Journalism & Mass Communication Quarterly* 92 (1): 142–160.
Blazer, Annie. 2019. "An Invitation to Suffer: Evangelicals and Sports Ministry in the U.S." *Religions* 10: 638.
Boateng, Godfred, David Teye Doku, Nancy Innocentia Ebu Enyan, Samuel Asiedu Owusu, Irene Korkoi Aboh, Ruby Victoria Kodom, Benard Ekumah, Reginald Quansah, Sheila A. Boamah, Dorcas Obiri-Yeboah, Epaphrodite Nsabimana, Stefan Jansen, and Frederick Ato Armah. 2021. "Prevalence and Changes in Boredom, Anxiety, and Well-Being Among Ghanaians During the COVID-19 Pandemic: A Population-Based Study." *BMC Public Health* 21: 1–13.
Borden, Iain. 2019. *Skateboarding and The City: A Complete History.* New York, NY: Bloomsbury.
Borish, Linda J. 2019. "Jewish Girls, Gender, and Sport at the Chicago Hebrew Institute: Athletic Identity in Jewish and Cultural Spaces." *Journal of Jewish Identities* 12(2): 149–173.
Borish, Linda J. 2002. "Women, Sport, and American Jewish Identity in the Late Nineteenth and Early Twentieth Centuries," in *With God on Their Side: Sport in the Service of Religion* edited by Tara Magdalinksi and Timothy Chandler. London: Routledge, pp. 71–98.
Brockhaus, Hannah. 2016. "Who Benefits from Sports? Everyone, Pope Francis Says," *CNA.* https://www.catholicnewsagency.com/news/34690/who-benefits-from-sports-everyone-pope-francis-says.
Brooks, Alison Wood, Juliana Schroeder, Jane L. Risen, Francesca Gino, Adam D. Galinsky, Michael I. Norton, and Maurice E. Schweitzer. 2016. "Don't Stop Believing: Rituals Improve Performance by Decreasing Anxiety," *Organizational Behavior and Human Decision Processes* 137: 71–85.
Broughton, David. 2022. "Participation Numbers, Gear Prices Grow," *Sports Business Journal.* Found at https://www.sportsbusinessjournal.com/Journal/Issues/2022/06/13/Portfolio/Research.aspx.
Brueggemann, Walter. 1978. *The Prophetic Imagination.* Philadelphia, PA: Fortress Press.
Bryant, Howard. 2018. *The Heritage: Black Athletes, a Divided America, and the Politics of Patriotism.* Boston, MA: Beacon Press.
Chan, Melissa. 2016. "Read LeBron James and Carmelo Anthony's Powerful Speech on Race at the ESPY Award." *Time.* https://time.com/4406289/lebron-james-carmelo-anthony-espy-awards-transcript/
Colás, Yago. 2016. *Ball Don't Lie. Myth, Genealogy, and Invention in the Cultures of Basketball.* Philadelphia, PA: Temple University Press.
Cooky, Cheryl and Michael Messner. 2018. *No Slam Dunk: Gender, Sport, and the Unevenness of Social Change.* Newark, NJ: Rutgers University Press.

Cooper, Joseph, Charles Macaulay, and Saturnino H. Rodriguez. 2019. "Race and Resistance: A Typology of African American Sport Activism," *International Review for the Sociology of Sport* 54 (2): 151–181.

Costa, Gustavo, José Afonso, Erika Brant, and Isabel Mesquita. 2012. "Differences in Game Patterns Between Male and Female Youth Volleyball," *Kinesiology* 44 (1): 60–66.

Cressler, Matthew. 2021. "A Secular Civil Rights Movement?: How Black Power and Black Catholics Help Us Rethink the Religion in Black Lives Matter," in *Race, Religion, and Black Lives Matter: Essays on a Moment and a Movement* edited by Christopher Cameron and Phillip Luke Sinitiere. Nashville, TN: Vanderbilt University Press.

Cummins, Robert A. 1996. "The Domains of Life Satisfaction: An Attempt to Order Chaos." *Social Indicators Research* 38 (3): 303–328.

Dann, Lori and Tracy Everbach. 2016. "Opening the Sports Closet: Media Coverage of the Self-Outings of Jason Collins and Brittney Griner," *Journal of Sports Media*, 11 (1): 169–192.

Dart, Jon. 2021. "Sport and British Jewish Identity," *International Review for the Sociology of Sport* 56 (5): 677–694.

Deb, Sopan. 2018. "Ibtihaj Muhammad: The Olympic Fencer Is Charting Her Own Path," *The New York Times*. https://www.nytimes.com/2018/07/24/books/ibtihaj-muhammad-fencing-hijab-olympics.html.

Dömötör, Zsuzsanna, Roberto Ruíz-Barquín and Attila Szabo. 2016. "Superstitious Behavior in Sport: A Literature Review," *Scandinavian Journal of Psychology* 57: 368–382.

Dorsch, Travis, Alan Smith, and Meghan McDonough. 2015. "Early Socialization of Parents Through Organized Youth Sport," *Sport, Exercise, and Performance Psychology* 14, 2157–3905.

Douglas, Karen, Joseph E. Uscinski, Robbie M. Sutton, Aleksandra Cichocka, Turkay Nefes, Chee Siang Ang, and Farzin Deravi. 2019. "Understanding Conspiracy Theories," *Advances in Political Psychology* 40 (1): 3–35.

Doyle, Jason P., Yiran Su, and Thilo Kunkel. 2020. "Athlete Branding Via Social Media: Examining the Factors Influencing Consumer Engagement on Instagram," *European Sport Management Quarterly*.

Drescher, Elizabeth. 2016. *Choosing Our Religion: The Spiritual Lives of America's Nones*. Oxford: Oxford University Press.

Duncan, Samuel. 2022. "The Spirit of Play: Fun and Freedom in the Professional Age of Sport." *Sports, Ethics, and Philosophy* 16 (3), 281–299.

Duriga, Joyce. 2016. "Mass at Wrigley Field? This Priest Holds It Every Week for the Cubs," *America: The Jesuit Review*. https://www.americamagazine.org/faith/2016/10/28/mass-wrigley-field-priest-holds-it-every-week-cubs.

Durkheim, Emile. 1912. *The Elementary Forms of Religious Life*. Translated by Karen Fields 1995. New York, NY: The Free Press.

Edwards, Harry. 2017. *The Revolt of the Black Athlete: 50th Anniversary Edition*. Urbana, IL: University of Illinois Press.

Eliade, Mircea. 1959. *The Sacred and the Profane*. Translated by William R. Trask. New York: Harcourt, Brace and Company, Inc.

Ellis, Robert. 2014. *The Games People Play: Theology, Religion, and Sport*. Eugene, OR: Wipf & Stock.

European Commission. 2022. "*Sport and Physical Activity*," April-May 2022. Found at https://europa.eu/eurobarometer/surveys/detail/2668.

Forbes, Bruce David and Jeffrey H. Mahan. 2017. *Religion and Popular Culture in America, 3rd Edition*. Oakland, CA: University of California Press.

Galily, Yair. 2019. "Shut Up and Dribble!"? Athletes Activism in the Age of Twittersphere: The Case of LeBron James," *Technology in Society* 58: 1–4.

Geertz, Clifford. 1993. *Religion as a Cultural System*. London: Tavistock.

Giulianotti, Richard. 2005. *Sport: A Critical Sociology*. Cambridge: Polity Press.

Giza, Christopher C., Mayumi L. Prins, David A. Hovda. 2017. "It's Not All Fun and Games: Sports, Concussions, and Neuroscience," *Neuron* 94: 1051–1055.

Glebova, Ekaterina, Fateme Zare, Michel Desbordes, and Gábor Géczi. 2022. "COVID-19 Sports Transformation: New Challenges and New Opportunities," *Physical Culture and Sport. Studies and Research* 95: 54–67.

"Global Views on Sports and Exercise," *Ipsos Global Advisors*, July 2021. Found at https://www.ipsos.com/sites/default/files/ct/news/documents/2021-08/Global%20views%20on%20sports%20and%20exercise%20Global%20Advisor.pdf.

Goffman, Erving. 1959. *The Presentation of the Self in Everyday Life*. New York, NY: Anchor Books.

Gomez, Jesus. 2016. "Carmelo Anthony is Organizing a Meeting with Community Leaders to Discuss Police-Related Shootings," *SBNation*. Found at https://www.sbnation.com/2016/7/22/12257790/carmelo-anthony-police-shooting-meeting-espys-speech.

Greenwood, Tracey and Teresa Delgado. 2011. "A Journey Toward Wholeness, a Journey to God: Physical Fitness as Embodied Spirituality." *Journal of Religion and Health* 52: 941–954.

Grix, Jonathan, Paul Michael Brannagan, Holly Grimes, and Ross Neville. 2020. "The Impact of COVID-19 on Sport," *International Journal of Sport Policy and Politics*: 1–12.

Hagan, John Elvis and Thomas Schack. 2019. "Integrating Pre-game Rituals and Pre-performance Routines in a Culture-specific Context: Implications for Sport Psychology Consultancy," *International Journal of Sport and Exercise Psychology* 17 (1): 18–31.

Hervieu-Leger, Danille. 2000. *Religion as a Chain of Memory*. Translated by Simon Lee. Cambridge: Polity Press.

Higgs, Robert and Michael Braswell. 2004. *An Unholy Alliance: The Sacred and Modern Sport*. Macon, GA: Mercer University Press.

Holt, Nicholas L., Kacey C. Neely, Linda G. Slater, Martin Camiré, Jean Côté, Jessica Fraser-Thomas, Dany MacDonald, Leisha Strachan, and Katherine A. Tamminen. 2017. "A Grounded Theory of Positive Youth Development Through Sport Based on Results From a Qualitative Meta-Study," *International Review of Sport and Exercise Psychology* 10 (1): 1–49.

Huizinga, Johan. 2016. *Homo Ludens: A Study of the Play-Element in Culture*. Kettering, OH: Angelica Press.

James, William. 1982. *The Varieties of Religious Experience*. New York, NY: Penguin Books.

Jones, Maya. 2022. "Disqualified for Running in a Hijab, Noor Alexandria Abukaram Turned Pain into Action." *ESPNW*. https://www.espn.com/espnw/story/_/id/34015634/disqualified-running-hijab-noor-alexandria-abukaram-turned-pain-action.

Kahneman, Daniel. 2011. *Thinking, Fast and Slow*. New York, NY: Farrar, Straus and Giroux.

Kalman-Lamb, Nathan. 2021. "Imagined Communities of Fandom: Sport, Spectatorship, Meaning and Alienation in Late Capitalism," *Sport in Society* 24 (6): 922–936.

Kilpatrick, Amina. 2022. "The Historical Significance of Kyrie Irving's Athletic Dominance During Ramadan," *NPR*. https://www.npr.org/2022/05/02/1095734394/ramadan-nba-playoffs-kyrie-irving.

Kim, Wonyoung, Ho Mun Jun, Matthew Walker, and Dan Drane. 2015. "Evaluating the Perceived Social Impacts of Hosting Large-Scale Sport Tourism Events: Scale Development and Validation," *Tourism Management* 48: 21–32.

King, Richard. 1999. *Orientalism and Religion: Post-Colonial Theory, India, and 'the Mystic East.'* London: Routledge.

Klein, Shawn. 2016. *Defining Sport: Conceptions and Borderlines*. New York, NY: Lexington Books.

Koenig, Harold. 2008. "Concerns About Measuring 'Spirituality' in Research." *The Journal of Nervous and Mental Disease* 196 (5): 349–355.

Legg, Eric, Mary Wells, Aubrey Newland, and Preston Tanner. 2017. "Exploring Sense of Community in Adult Recreational Tennis," *World Leisure Journal*, 59 (1): 39–53.

Lehr, Steven A., Meghan L. Ferreira, and Mahzarin R. Banaji. 2019. "When Outgroup Negativity Trumps Ingroup Positivity: Fans of the Boston Red Sox and New York Yankees Place Greater Value on Rival Losses Than Own-Team Gains," *Group Processes & Intergroup Relations*, 22 (1): 26–42.

Lewis, Jerry. 2007. *Sports Fan Violence in North America*. New York, NY: Rowman & Littlefield Publishers, Inc.

Lowe, Zach. 2020. "Pope Francis Hosts NBA Players to Talk Social Justice," *ESPN*. https://www.espn.com/nba/story/_/id/30371187/nba-players-pope-meet-talk-social-justice.

Luckman, Thomas. 1967. *The Invisible Religion: The Problem of Religion in Modern Society*. New York, NY: MacMillan Publishing Company.

Luther, Jessica and Kavitha Davidson. 2020. *Loving Sports When They Don't Love You Back: Dilemmas of the Modern Fan*. New York, NY: University of Texas Press.

Magdalinksi, Tara and Timothy Chandler. 2002. "With God on Their Side: An Introduction," in *With God on Their Side: Sport in the Service of Religion* edited by Tara Magdalinksi and Timothy Chandler. London: Routledge, pp. 1–19.

Magrath, Rory. 2022. *Athlete Activism: Contemporary Perspectives*. Abingdon: Taylor & Francis Group.

Mann, Robert, Bryan Clift, Jules Boykoff, and Sheree Bekker. 2020. "Athletes as Community; Athletes in Community: COVID-19, Sporting Mega-events and Athlete Health Protection," *British Journal of Sports Medicine* 54: 1071–1072.

Manning, Christel. 2015. *Losing Our Religion: How Unaffiliated Parents are Raising Their Children*. New York, NY: New York University Press.

Martín, Eloísa. 2018. "Soccer Fandom as Catechism: Practices of the Sacred Among Young Men in Argentina," in *Global Perspectives on Sports and Christianity* edited by Afe Adogame, Nick J. Watson, and Andrew Parker. New York, NY: Routledge.

Marx, Karl. 1970. *A Contribution to the Critique of Hegel's 'Philosophy of Right.'* Translated by Annette Jolin and Joseph O'Malley. Cambridge: Cambridge University Press.

Masuzawa, Tomoko. 2005. *The Invention of World Religions*. Chicago, IL: University of Chicago Press.

Matias, Cristino J. A., Jara González-Silva, M. Perla Moreno, and Pablo J. Greco. 2021. "Performance Analysis of U19 Male and Female Setters in the Brazilian Volleyball Championship Teams," *Kinesiology* 53 (1): 113–121.

Miner, Horace. 1956. "Body Ritual Among the Nacirema," *American Anthropologist* 58 (3): 503–507.

Monis, Khan. 2018. "Hakeem Olajuwon's Five Most Impressive Ramadan Performances," *Andscape*. https://andscape.com/features/hakeem-olajuwons-most-impressive-ramadan-performances/.

Moore, Louis. 2017. *We Will Win the Day: The Civil Rights Movement, the Black Athlete, and the Quest for Equality*. Santa Barbara, CA: Praeger.

Muhammad, Ibtihaj. 2018. *Proud: My Fight for an Unlikely American Dream*. New York, NY: LegacyLit.

Mwaniki, Munene F. 2019. "Islam and the Foreign Other: Representing the Alterity of Hakeem Olajuwon," in *Sports in African History, Politics, and Identity Formation*, edited by Michael J. Gennaro, and Saheed Aderinto. Abingdon: Taylor & Francis Group, pp. 220–252.

Ncube, Lyton. 2017. "Visualizing Diverse Religious Performances: The 'Sacred' and the 'Profane' in Zimbabwean Football." *Critical Arts* 31 (4): 39–88.

Norman, Jim. 2018. "The Religious Regions of the U.S." *Gallup*. https://news.gallup.com/poll/232223/religious-regions.aspx.

Norwood, Stephen A. 2009. "'American Jewish Muscle': Forging a New Masculinity in the Streets and in the Ring 1890–1940," *Modern Judaism* 29 (2): 167–193.

O'Connor, Paul. 2017. "Handrails, Steps, and Curbs: Sacred Places and Secular Pilgrimage in Skateboarding." *Sport in Society* 21: 1651–1668.

O'Connor, Paul. 2019. *Skateboarding and Religion*. Switzerland: Palgrave MacMillan.

O'Reilly, David. 2018. "When You Say You Believe in God, What Do You Mean?" Found at https://www.pewtrusts.org/en/trust/archive/fall-2018/when-you-say-you-believe-in-god-what-do-you-mean.

Olajuwon, Hakeem with Knobler, Peter. 1996. *Living the Dream: My Life and Basketball*. Boston, MA: Little, Brown and Company.

Otto, Rudolph. 1958. *The Idea of the Holy*. Oxford: Oxford University Press.

Owton, Helen and Andrew C. Sparkes. 2017. "Sexual Abuse and the Grooming Process in Sport: Learning from Bella's Story," *Sport, Education and Society* 22 (6): 732–743.

Parent, Sylvie, Francine Lavoie, Marie-Ève Thibodeau, Martine Hébert, Martin Blais, and Team PAJ. 2016. "Sexual Violence Experienced in the Sport Context by a Representative Sample of Quebec Adolescents," *Journal of Interpersonal Violence* 31 (16): 2666–2686.

Pew Research Center. 2021. "About Three-in-Ten U.S. Adults are Now Religious Unaffiliated." https://www.pewresearch.org/religion/2021/12/14/about-three-in-ten-u-s-adults-are-now-religiously-unaffiliated/.

Pew Research Center. 2018. "Being Christian in Western Europe." https://www.pewresearch.org/religion/2018/05/29/beliefs-about-god/.

Pew Research Center. 2017. "The Growth of Germany's Muslim Population." https://www.pewresearch.org/religion/2017/11/29/the-growth-of-germanys-muslim-population-2/.

Pew Research Center. 2018. "When Americans Say They Believe in God, What Do They Mean?" https://www.pewresearch.org/religion/2018/04/25/when-americans-say-they-believe-in-god-what-do-they-mean/.

Price, Joseph L. 2001. *From Season to Season: Sports as American Religion*. Macon, GA: Mercer University Press.

Pu, Haozhou, Jeeyoon Kim, and Corinne Daprano. 2021. "Can Esports Substitute Traditional Sports? The Convergence of Sports and Video Gaming During the Pandemic and Beyond." *Societies* 11: 1–18.

Public Research on Religion. 2021. "The 2020 Census of American Religion." July 8. https://www.prri.org/research/2020-census-of-american-religion/.

Raine, Susan and Stephen A. Kent. (2019). "The Grooming of Children for Sexual Abuse in Religious Settings: Unique Characteristics and Select Case Studies," *Aggression and Violent Behavior* 48: 180–189.

Renaud, Myriam and Lerone Jonathan Wilder. 2021. "Black Lives Matter: Where are the Black Clergy," *Aljazeera*. Found at https://www.aljazeera.com/features/2021/2/24/black-lives-matter-where-are-the-black-clergy.

Rhoden, William. 2006. *Forty Million Dollar Slaves: The Rise, Fall, and Redemption of the Black Athlete*. New York, NY: Three Rivers Press.

Roof, Wade Clark. 1999. *Spiritual Marketplace: Baby Boomers and the Remaking of American Religion*. Princeton, NJ: Princeton University Press.

Ruihley, Brody, Andrew Billings, and Nick Buzzelli. 2021. "A Swiftly Changing Tide: Fantasy Sport, Gambling, and Alternative Forms of Participation." *Games and Culture* 16 (6): 681–701.

Sage, George. 2010. *Globalizing Sport: How Organizations, Corporations, Media, and Politics are Changing Sport*. New York: Routledge.

Samuels, Jeffrey. 2010. *Attracting the Heart: Social Relations and the Aesthetics of Emotion in Sri Lankan Monastic Culture*. Honolulu, HI: University of Hawai'i Press.

Sayles, Damon. 2023. "Jason Collins, 10 Years After Coming Out, on LGBTQ+ in Sports, the NHL and More," *The Athletic*. Found at https://theathletic.com/4489473/2023/05/08/jason-collins-lgbtq-issues-representation-sports/.

Scholes, Jeffrey and Raphael Sassower. 2014. *Religion and Sports in American Culture*. New York, NY: Routledge.

Schwartz, Barry. 2004. *The Paradox of Choice: Why More is Less*. New York, NY: HarperCollins Publishers.

Serazio, Michael. 2019. *The Power of Sports: Media and Spectacle in American Culture*. New York, NY: New York University Press.

Sheldrake, Philip. 2012. *Spirituality: A Very Short Introduction*. Oxford: Oxford University Press.
Shkurko, Alexander. 2014. "Cognitive Mechanisms of Ingroup/Outgroup Distinction," *Journal for the Theory of Social Behaviour* 45 (2): 188–213.
Shoemaker, Terry. 2018. *The Prophetic Dimension of Sport*. Cham, Switzerland: Springer.
Shoemaker, Terry. 2019. "Deconversion, Sport, and Rehabilitative Hope," *Religions* 10.
Shoemaker, Terry. 2023a. "Sport, Religion, and Absence: The Subfield of Religion and Sport as an Explanatory Tool for the Moment," in *Religion and Sports in North America: Critical Essays for the Twenty-First Century*, edited by Jeffrey Scholes and Randall Balmer, pp. 121–133.
Shoemaker, Terry. 2023b. "Sport as Spirituality?: Direct and Indirect Methodologies and Considerations," *International Journal of Sport and Religion* 1 (2): 47–69.
Shoemaker, Terry and Ciara Bernal. 2024. "Skateboarding and Subjective-Life Embodied Spirituality." *Journal of Contemporary Religion*. Forthcoming.
Sims, Megan. 2021. "Olympic Fencer Ibtihaj Muhammad Says 'Religious Freedom is a Human Right' After Proposed France Hijab Ban." *Yahoo! Life*. https://www.yahoo.com/lifestyle/ibtihaj-muhammad-says-religious-freedom-france-hijab-ban-154036813.html.
Smart, Ninian. 1998. *The World's Religions*. Cambridge: Cambridge University Press.
Spaaij, Ramón, Karen Farquharson, and Timothy Marjoribanks. 2015. "Sport and Social Inequalities," *Sociology Compass* 9 (5): 400–411.
Stark, Rodney and William Bainbridge. 1996. *A Theory of Religion*. New Brunswick, NJ: Rutgers University Press.
Sullivan, Emily. 2018. "Laura Ingraham Told LeBron James To Shut Up And Dribble; He Went To The Hoop," *NPR*. Found at https://www.npr.org/sections/thetwo-way/2018/02/19/587097707/laura-ingraham-told-lebron-james-to-shutup-and-dribble-he-went-to-the-hoop.
Tebow, Tim. 2013. *Through My Eyes*. New York, NY: HarperOne.
Telford, Rohan M., Richard D. Telford, Thomas Cochrane, Ross B. Cunningham, Lisa S. Olive, and Rachel Davey. 2016. "The Influence of Sport Club Participation on Physical Activity, Fitness and Body Fat During Childhood and Adolescence: The LOOK Longitudinal Study," *Journal of Science and Medicine in Sport* 19 (5): 400–406.
Thorpe, Holly, Kim Toffoletti, and Toni Bruce. 2017. "Sportswomen and Social Media: Bringing Third-Wave Feminism, Postfeminism, and Neoliberal Feminism Into Conversation," *Journal of Sport and Social Issues* 41 (5): 359–383.

Tucker, Tim and Noel Woodbridge. 2012. "Motivational Factors for a Sports Ministry: A Case Study of Churches in Pretoria," *Theological Studies* 68 (2): 1–7.

Vamplew, Wray. 2021. *Games People Played: A Global History of Sport*. London: Reaktion Books.

Wacker, Grant. 2014. *America's Pastor: Billy Graham and the Shaping of a Nation*. Cambridge, MA: Harvard University Press.

Walker, Grant. 2014. *America's Pastor: Billy Graham and the Shaping of a Nation*. Cambridge, MA: Harvard University Press.

Weber, Max. 1922. *The Sociology of Religion*. Boston, MA: Beacon Press.

Weber, Max. 1930. *The Protestant Ethic and the Spirit of Capitalism*. New York: Routledge.

Wessels, Marlene, Nariman Utegaliyev, Christoph Bernhard, Robin Welsch, Daniel Oberfeld, Sven Thönes, and Christoph von Castell. 2022. "Adapting to the Pandemic: Longitudinal Effects of Social Restrictions on Time Perception and Boredom During the COVID-19 Pandemic in Germany." *Scientific Reports* 12: 1–12.

Westmattelmann, Daniel, Jan-Gerrit Grotenhermen, Marius Sprenger, and Gerhard Schewe. 2020. "The Show Must Go On – Virtualisation of Sport Events During the COVID-19 Pandemic," *European Journal of Information System*: 119–136.

Wonyoung Kim, Ho Mun Jun, Matthew Walker, and Dan Drane. 2015. "Evaluating the Perceived Social Impacts of Hosting Large-Scale Sport Tourism Events: Scale Development and Validation," *Tourism Management* 48: 21–32.

Woodbine, Onaje X.O. 2016. *Black Gods of the Asphalt: Religion, Hip-Hop, and Street Basketball*. New York, NY: Columbia University Press.

Yan, Linlin, Yiqun Gan, Xu Ding, Jianhui Wu, and Hongxia Duan. 2021. The Relationship Between Perceived Stress and Emotional Distress During the COVID-19 Outbreak: Effects of Boredom Proneness and Coping Style. *Journal of Anxiety Disorders* 77: 1–11.

Young, Tunde. 2022. "How Nigerian basketball legend Hakeem Olajuwon used to dominate the NBA during Ramadan," *Pulse Sports*. https://www.pulse.ng/sports/basketball/how-nigerian-basketball-legend-hakeem-olajuwon-used-to-dominate-the-nba-during/f6ywvqy.

Zinnbauer, Brian J., Kenneth I. Pargament, Brenda Cole, Mark S. Rye, Eric M. Butter, Timothy G. Belavich, Kathleen M. Hipp, Allie B. Scott, and Jill L. Kader. 1997. "Religion and Spirituality: Unfuzzying the Fuzzy." *Journal for the Scientific Study of Religion* 36 (4): 549–564.

INDEX

Abdul-Rauf, Mahmoud 38
Abdullah, Husain 32–33, 36
Abukaram, Noor Alexandria 41
activism 60, 107–108, 111–112, 120, 148
Ali, Muhammad 36–37, 39, 107, 147
Alpert, Rebecca 38, 41, 48, 65
antisemitism 64, 66, 68
athlete 26, 29–35, 42, 45, 47, 51, 69, 91, 100, 103, 107–108, 113–120, 151

Bain-Selbo, Eric 87, 93, 155, 162
Bainbridge Island 78–81, 83, 93, 95, 125, 137, 139–140, 142, 144
Baltimore Ravens 2–4, 7–8
baseball 30–31, 33, 35, 67, 76, 84, 88–89, 93, 97, 102, 118, 137, 158, 163
basketball 9–10, 19, 26, 37–39, 47, 51, 58–59, 66, 82, 93, 97, 99, 101–102, 108–109, 113–115, 117, 124, 156, 158, 163
beliefs 4, 13, 32, 34, 39, 63, 77, 125, 139, 156, 162
Berger, Peter 153–154, 156, 166–168
BLM (Black Lives Matter) 109–113
Borish, Linda 65
boxing 18, 36, 66
Brueggemann, Walter 108–111
Buddhism 75, 77, 82, 97

capitalism 21, 90, 127, 136, 143–144, 151
Christian 2, 6–7, 9, 12, 18, 27, 32, 34–35, 41, 43, 45, 49, 57–61, 63, 69, 72, 86–88, 93, 101, 108, 111, 113, 115, 137, 156, 159
Christianity 6, 9, 11–12, 18, 33, 56, 59–60, 63, 67–68, 70, 72, 75, 82, 92–93, 106, 111, 161
church 2–3, 7, 16–17, 56–58, 82, 98, 112–113, 119, 137
coaches 19, 41, 58, 98, 101–102, 121, 151, 162
colonialism 6, 12–13, 15, 19, 22–23, 63, 67, 72, 92–93
COVID-19 20, 145, 153–155, 158–159, 162–164, 166–167
cricket 68, 96–97
CWF (Christian Wrestling Association) 58–59

definition (of religion) 6–7, 10, 12, 14–15
deity or deities 7, 10–12, 27, 31, 75–77, 83, 85–86, 146–147, 153
devotees 102, 104–105, 107, 132, 147
devotion 7, 18–20, 29–33, 35–36, 38–39, 44–47, 53, 75–76, 83, 92, 100, 104–105, 115, 119, 136, 140–141, 146–148, 151, 161, 165, 167
disenchantment 19, 90–91, 95

Durkheim, Émile 161–162, 166

economics 4, 21, 27, 74, 83, 106
Eliade, Mircea 76, 80–81, 146, 157, 166
entertainment 59, 74, 124, 161, 166
equality 19, 102, 108, 110, 116–117
ESPN 36, 109, 114–115
ESPYs 109–110

fandom 7, 17, 21, 23, 50, 52, 82, 124, 148–149, 156, 163–164
fans 3–4, 7, 14–15, 17, 20–21, 26, 32–34, 38–40, 44–47, 49, 52–53, 58–59, 62, 75–76, 88–89, 92, 100–101, 103, 105, 111, 113–115, 121, 123–124, 129, 147, 149–150, 155, 158–159, 161–164
fencing 41
FIFA 52, 161
football 3, 7, 15, 17, 26, 31, 33–34, 39, 58–59, 67, 76, 82, 92–94, 96, 101, 104, 109, 156, 158–159, 161–162

Geertz, Clifford 13
gender 4, 9, 19, 42, 52, 54, 65, 68, 102, 107–108, 116–118, 120, 135, 137, 140, 165
god/gods 10–12, 32, 86, 89
Goffman, Erving 113
golf 18, 65
Graham, Billy 55–56, 59
Griner, Brittney 108, 116

hijab 40–41, 47
Hindu 1, 11–12, 21, 27, 97, 101, 137
hockey 26, 67, 96, 124, 141
homo ludens 84–86
homo religiosus 83, 89, 91–95, 150
Huizinga, Johan 84–85

inequalities 19, 102, 120, 154–155
Ingroup 62–70, 101
intersectionality 116–119
Islam 11, 21, 26, 36–41, 47, 67–68, 82, 93, 106, 111, 147

James, William 163–164
Jewish 8, 18, 35, 41, 49, 64–71, 80, 86, 106, 137
Judaism 11, 21, 93, 97
judo 41
justice 19, 105, 110, 113, 115, 117

Luckman, Thomas 6–7

Marx, Karl 146, 154–156, 166
Masuzawa, Tomoko 12, 23
Mircea 76, 80, 146, 157
Muhammed, Ibtihaj 40, 47
Muslim 5, 12, 18, 21, 26, 32, 35, 37–42, 47, 71, 80, 93, 101, 137, 147

Nacirema 159–160
NBA 19, 37–38, 102, 110, 112, 114–115, 119, 148, 158, 163
NFL 31–33, 38, 52, 92, 109, 159
NHL 52
Nongbri, Brent 23

O'Connor, Paul 129, 144
Olajuwon, Hakeem 37–39, 46–47, 147
Olympics 128, 153, 168
Otto, Rudolph 146, 163–164
outgroup 62–63, 66–67, 70, 101

pandemic 20, 145, 149–150, 154–156, 158–159, 162–168
pickleball 16, 19–20, 75–76, 78–83, 95, 137, 139–143
pilgrimage 81, 93, 95
play 14–15, 19–20, 50–51, 55, 58–59, 64–66, 69–71, 84–86, 139–140, 153, 158, 162, 168
Poe, Edgar Allen 2–4, 7–8, 17
prayer 9, 16, 30, 32–33, 40, 42, 45, 49, 56
Price, Joseph 88–89, 157
prophetic 19, 80, 105–113, 119
proselytization 18, 55, 57–59, 61, 63, 68–71

qualitative research 5, 10, 20, 122, 129, 133–135, 140–144
quantitative research 5, 10, 20, 122, 137, 141–144

race 19, 101–102, 107, 112, 116–120, 155
racism 108, 112, 148
Ramadan 18, 37, 147
ritual 3–4, 6–8, 12–13, 17, 21, 27, 30, 34, 44–45, 63, 71, 74, 77, 80–82, 85–89, 92–93, 98, 100–101, 147, 149–150, 153, 157, 159–160, 163, 166–168

sacred canopy 153, 167–168
Santa Fe 137, 139–140
secular 18, 42–47, 49, 108, 113, 119, 147
sexuality 19, 105, 107, 115–117
Shahrkhani, Ali Seraj Abdulrahim 41
skateboarding 20, 128–134, 144
Smart, Ninian 13
soccer 21, 26, 30, 34, 38, 51, 58, 67–68, 71, 76, 82, 84, 93, 101, 108, 124–125, 141

social media 32, 34–35, 53, 61–62, 98, 108, 113–119
spirituality 20, 34–35, 111, 126–127, 130–133, 139–144, 165
Strawberry, Darryl 35
supernatural 28, 31, 63, 100, 154
superstitious 3, 17, 30, 149
surfing 58, 128

Tebow, Tim 31–33, 35–36, 39, 46–47
tennis 16, 78–79, 94, 107
transcendence 93–94, 112, 129
transcendent 28, 82–83, 93

uniforms 40–41, 52, 61, 89

violence 19, 93–94, 100–104, 109–110
volleyball 51, 55, 84, 94, 124

Weber, Max 90–91, 106–108
WNBA 66, 102, 107, 109–110, 115–116, 163
wrestling 59, 61

For Product Safety Concerns and Information please contact our EU representative GPSR@taylorandfrancis.com
Taylor & Francis Verlag GmbH, Kaufingerstraße 24, 80331 München, Germany

www.ingramcontent.com/pod-product-compliance
Lightning Source LLC
Chambersburg PA
CBHW050526170426
43201CB00013B/2106